Word into Silence

Other books by John Main available from
Canterbury Press

Monastery Without Walls: The Spiritual Letters of John Main
Edited by Laurence Freeman OSB
Complete and unabridged edition

Door to Silence
Edited and introduced by Laurence Freeman OSB
Drawn from John Main's talks and group meditations

www.canterburypress.co.uk

Word into Silence

John Main

Edited by
Laurence Freeman

CANTERBURY
PRESS
Norwich

© The World Community for Christian Meditation 2006

First published in Great Britain in 1980 by
Darton, Longman & Todd

This edition published in 2006 by
the Canterbury Press Norwich
(a publishing imprint of Hymns Ancient & Modern Limited,
a registered charity)
9–17 St Alban's Place, London N1 0NX

www.scm-canterburypress.co.uk

British Library Cataloguing in Publication data

A catalogue record for this book is available
from the British Library

ISBN 1-85311-754-1/9781-85311-754-4

Typeset by Regent Typesetting, London
Printed and bound in Great Britain
by William Clowes Ltd, Beccles, Suffolk

Contents

Preface

The beauty of the Christian vision of life is its vision of unity. It sees that all mankind has been unified in the One who is in union with the Father. All matter, all creation, too, is drawn into the cosmic movement towards unity that will be the realization of the Divine harmony. This is not an abstract vision. It is filled with a deep personal joy because within it the value of each person is affirmed. No unique beauty will be lost in this great unification but each will be brought to fulfilment in all. In union we become who we are called to be. Only in union do we know fully who we are.

This is the great controlling vision that has steered the Christian tradition for centuries. Without it we cannot call ourselves His disciples. And yet it is the task of each of us to grow up into this vision in our personal experience, to see it for ourselves, or rather, to see it with the eyes of our Lord. The central task of our life, in the Christian vision, is to come into union, into communion. Putting this from the point of view where most of us start, it means going beyond all dualism, all dividedness within ourselves and beyond the alienation separating us from others. It was dualism that characterized the heresies that threatened to destroy the fine centrality, the balance of the Christian perspective. It is dualism, too, that creates for each of us the impossible, unrealistic 'either-ors' that cause so much unnecessary anguish: God or humanity, love of self or love of neighbour, cloister or market place.

To communicate the Christian experience of union, the experience of God in Jesus, we have to resolve these false dichotomies, first of all, in ourselves. We have to be made one by the One who is one.

It seems to be the nature of dualities to propagate themselves and so to complicate the wholeness and simplicity from which we start and to which deep prayer recalls us. One of the most fundamental of these dualities has been the polarization of the active and contemplative life, and its most harmful effect has been to alienate the majority of Christians from that same deep prayer which transcends complexity and restores unity. We came to think of ourselves as either contemplative or active, and this distinction held for religious as well as the laity. As an active we were among the vast majority whose spiritual life rested on the devotional, or the intellectual, and who made no presumptuous claim to an experience of God. As a contemplative, we were part of a small, privileged minority, separated from the main body not only by high walls and strange customs but often by specialized vocabularies or even total non-communication.

Like all heresies this one proved plausible and lasting because it possessed a grain of truth. There *are* some who are called to live in the Spirit on the margin of the world's busyness and whose primary values are silence, stillness and solitude. The contemplatives are not preachers, perhaps, but they must nevertheless communicate their experience because their experience is self-communicating. Their experience is the experience of love and love reaches out to communicate, to share, to widen the realm of its own communion. The conclusion drawn from the false understanding of the Church's contemplative dimension distorted the explicit teaching of the New Testament, namely, that the call to sanctity is universal. The call of the Absolute is made to each of us and it is only this call that gives us ultimate meaning; our ultimate value is the freedom we are given to respond to it. The exclusion of the majority of Christians from this call had deep and major effects on both Church and Society. If our ultimate value and meaning is denied, how can we expect a human reverence for each other to be the guiding principle of our ordinary relations?

There is no greater need in the Church and in the world today than for the renewed understanding that the call to prayer, to deep prayer, is universal. Unity among Christians as well as, in the long term, unity among different races and creeds rests upon our finding the inner principle of unity as a personal experience within our own hearts. If we are to realize that Christ is indeed the peace between us, we have to know that 'Christ is all and is in all'. And we in Him. The authority with which the Church communicates this experience will be the degree to which we, the Church and Christ's Body, have realized it personally. Our authority has to be humble, that is, it has to be rooted in an experience that takes us beyond ourselves into full personhood. Our authority as disciples is our closeness to the Author, far removed from authoritarianism or that complex of fear and guilt by which power is used by man against man. Christians, in their prayer, renounce their own power. They leave self behind. In so doing, they place absolute faith in the power of Christ as the only power that increases the unity among all human beings because it is the power of love, the power of union itself. As Christian men and women of prayer open their hearts to this power they enlarge the capacity of all people to find the peace that lies beyond their ordinary understanding.

It is not a new idea that Christians should pray. The really contemporary challenge is that we should recover a way of deep prayer that will lead us into the experience of union, away from the surface distractions and self-piety. The questions today have always been there: How do we pray at this level? How do we learn the discipline it involves? How do we concentrate ourselves, in a wholly natural way, in the deepest reality of our faith? How do we make the essential transition from imagination to reality, from the conceptual to the concrete, from notional assent to personal experience? It is not enough to approach these questions as intellectual problems. They are far more urgent than that. They are challenges to our existence and so they can only be answered, not by ideas, but with our life.

The simplest way to answer the question, 'How do we pray?' can be found in St Paul's statement: 'We do not even know how we ought to pray, but the Spirit prays within us.' The Christian has been given freedom from all problematical questions about prayer by the revelation that what he calls 'his prayer' is nothing less than an entry into the prayer-experience of Jesus himself, the Spirit, the bond of union with the Father. It is this personal experience of Jesus that is the present, the eternally present reality at the heart of every human consciousness. All our seeking for secret knowledge, hidden ways or teaching has been rendered unnecessary because the ultimate secret has been revealed: 'the secret is this – Christ in you'. So, in prayer we are not striving to make something happen. It has already happened. We are simply realizing what already is, by travelling deeper into the unified consciousness of Jesus, into the wonder of our own creation. The prison of self-fixation that prevents our making this journey can no longer hold those who can understand that 'we possess the mind of Christ'.

When we understand that the centre of prayer is in Christ, not ourselves, then we can ask 'How?' and receive a useful answer. The journey we make to this point of departure is a first stage, and perhaps it will be a difficult, lonely journey. But at this moment in our life we awaken to ourselves within the community of all those others who have come to this same point and have travelled

on. Our own experience leads us into the tradition; in our acceptance of the tradition we make it live and pass it on to those who
follow us. What is important is that we recognize and embrace
the opportunity to make our own experience fully real.

The tradition of Christian meditation is a simple and, above
all, practical response to this question and yet within it is con-
centrated the rich and profound experience of the saints, known
and unknown. It is a tradition rooted in the teachings of Jesus,
the religious tradition in which he lived and taught, the Apostolic Church and the Fathers. Very soon in the Christian Church
it became a tradition associated with monks and monasticism
and ever since has been a principal channel through which it has
spread into the whole Body and nourished it. I do not think there
is anything mysterious about this. Monks are essentially men and
women whose first priority is practice rather than theory, whose
inner and outer poverty is designed to facilitate the 'experience-
in-itself' rather than reflection upon the experience. It is then
only natural, indeed inevitable, that meditation should be found
at the heart of monasticism. And, because it is found there,
monasticism is important to the Church and to the world.

Such a monasticism, clear as to its own priority, will be an
inclusive rather than an exclusive movement in the Church. It
will know that the experience has only to be really lived to be
communicated. Where the path is being followed by a few, others
will be drawn to it. Something will have to be said, written or
discussed. But the profoundest teaching and the end of all words
will be a participation in the creative moment of prayer. It is the
silence of monks that is their true eloquence.

People sometimes express concern about the availability of
the monastic tradition of meditation. In communicating it, they
wonder, are monks not saying that this is the only way? Behind
this, very often, is the fear that too absolute a demand is being
made on 'ordinary Christians', the 'non-contemplatives'. But

this is the demand, the opportunity, presented by the gospel to all men and women in every age and culture. It was to 'all' that Jesus revealed the condition for following him. The irony is that 'ordinary' people have been seeking this way outside the Church in their thousands, people who could not find this spiritual teaching in the Church when they went to find it, and so they have looked to the East or to forms of Eastern religion imported to the West. When such people hear of their own Western, Christian tradition of meditation they express astonishment: 'Why has this been kept from us?' they ask. The meeting of East and West in the Spirit, which is one of the great features of our time, can only be fruitful if it is realized on the level of deep prayer. This, surely, is also true of the union of the different Christian denominations. The precondition is that we rediscover the richness of our own tradition, and have the courage to embrace it.

But is all this merely religious utopianism? This book is based on the faith that it is not. And the faith is based on the experience we have had as a monastery in communicating and sharing this tradition as a living reality. In our Community we have as our priority four periods of meditation each day that are integrated with our Office and Eucharist. Beyond that, our work is to communicate and share our tradition with whoever wishes to be open to it. The majority of those coming to our weekly meditation groups or of those coming to stay with us as guests or to meditate with us at our communal times of prayer, are people with families, careers, the normal and demanding responsibilities of life. Yet meditation has spoken to them, created a space of silence in their lives each morning and each evening and provided them with structure and discipline in their search for depth and rootedness in Christ. To label them merely 'active' or 'contemplative' misses the point. They are people who have heard the gospel and who seek to respond at the deepest level of their being to the infinite gift they have received in the love of

God that comes to us in Jesus. They know that this response is a journey into the endless depths of God's love. They have simply begun to make that journey.

This book was stimulated by the response of these people to meditation. The substance of it is a set of tapes we made some years ago in England as an introduction to meditation and a means of encouragement to those who have begun to meditate, especially for those who could not visit or stay long with us. It began therefore with the spoken word and I think that remains the ideal means of communicating this tradition. The mystery into which meditation leads us is a personal mystery, the mystery of our own personhood, which finds its completion in the person of Christ. And so, the more personal the way it is communicated, the closer it is to its source and its goal.

So, I ask you to remember that the words printed in this book originally came to life as spoken words and I hope, in remembering this, they will speak to you from a tradition that must always come alive in our own experience.

John Main OSB
Montreal

Biography of John Main

John Main, one of the spiritual masters of our time, was born into an Irish family in England in 1926. He served briefly in the Royal Corps of Signals at the end of World War Two and then embarked on a period of training in religious life. Deciding it was not the time for vows he studied law in Ireland and then joined the British Diplomatic Service.

He was introduced to meditation while posted in Malaya, and began to integrate its practice into his Christian prayer. He returned to Europe and became Professor of International Law at Trinity College Dublin. In 1958 he became a Benedictine monk at Ealing Abbey in London and was advised to give up his practice of meditation; he complied, only to return to it, as he said in his autobiographical *The Gethsemani Talks*, 'on God's terms not my own' some years later.

He studied in Rome during the heady years of the Second Vatican Council and then returned to teach at the monastery's school in London. In 1969 he was sent to St Anselm's Abbey in Washington DC and here, through John Cassian and the Christian monastic desert tradition, he reconnected to the path of meditation. Increasingly conscious of the importance of this tradition of contemplative prayer for modern Christianity and the world, he formed a small lay community committed to its practice in community and integrated with traditional Benedictine monastic life.

At the invitation of the Archbishop of Montreal in 1977 he formed a new kind of Benedictine community of monks and lay people, based on the practice of Christian meditation and committed to teaching it as its primary work. His talks and retreats during the next period of his life formed the basis of his enduring influence on the spiritual life of contemporary Christianity. In *Word into Silence* he wrote a powerful and concise explanation of the meaning of Christian prayer in contemporary terms, true to the theological and mystical traditions and yet able to connect with the spiritual questions and searching of his time. His letters to the growing worldwide community of Christian meditators (*Monastery Without Walls*) opened up new dimensions of spiritual meaning within the tradition and in dialogue with other faiths. Through the spoken word in particular, such as his weekly talks at the monastery recorded as the *Communitas* series, his influence is still powerful in the formation of Christian meditation groups throughout the world. He died in Montreal on 30 December 1982.

How to Meditate

Sit down. Sit still and upright. Close your eyes lightly. Sit relaxed but alert. Silently, interiorly begin to say a single word. We recommend the prayer-phrase 'Maranatha'. Recite it as four syllables of equal length. Listen to it as you say it, gently but continuously. Do not think or imagine anything – spiritual or otherwise. If thoughts and images come, these are distractions at the time of meditation, so keep returning to simply saying the word. Meditate each morning and evening for between twenty and thirty minutes.

Introduction

L earning to meditate is not just a matter of mastering a technique. It is much more learning to appreciate and respond
directly to the depths of your own nature, not human nature in
general but your own in particular. Ideally, you should find a
teacher who will help to guide you on your pilgrimage. This little
book may inspire you to do that.

Being Restored to Ourselves

First we must understand the Christian context of meditation.
I am using the term meditation in this instance synonymously
with such terms as contemplation, contemplative prayer, meditative prayer, and so on. The essential context of meditation is to be
found in the fundamental relationship of our lives, the relationship that we have as creatures with God, our Creator. But most of
us have to take a preliminary step before we can begin to appreciate the full wonder and glorious mystery of this fundamental

relationship. Most of us have to get into touch with ourselves first, to get into a full relationship with ourselves before we can turn openly to our relationship with God. Putting this another way, we can say that we have first to find, expand and experience our own capacity for peace, for serenity, and for harmony before we can begin to appreciate our God and Creator who is the author of all harmony and serenity.

Meditation is the very simple process by which we prepare ourselves, in the first instance, to be at peace with ourselves so that we are capable of appreciating the peace of the Godhead within us. The view of meditation that many people are encouraged to take as a means of relaxation, of retaining inner peacefulness throughout the pressures of the modern urban life, is not essentially wrong in itself. But if this is all it is seen as being, the view is very limited because, as we become more and more relaxed in ourselves, and the longer we meditate, the more we become aware that the source of our new-found calm in our daily lives is precisely the life of God within us. The degree of peace we possess is directly proportional to our awareness of this fact of life, a fact of human consciousness, common to every man and every woman in the world. But to realize this fact as a present reality in our lives, we have to decide that we want to be at peace. This is the reason for the psalmist's saying: 'Be still and know that I am God' (Ps. 46.10).

This deep inner peacefulness is in a sense more freely available for us today than it was for the Hebrew poet who wrote that psalm, even if our problems are greater and our pace of life faster than his were; and this is because of the great fact of Jesus.

The great conviction of the New Testament is that Jesus by giving us His Spirit has dramatically transformed the fabric of human consciousness. Our redemption by Jesus Christ has opened up for us levels of consciousness that can be described by St Paul only in terms of a totally new creation. As a result of all that Jesus has accomplished for the humanity into whose being He fully entered, we have been quite literally re-created. In Chapter 5 of Paul's letter to the Romans he writes about what God has accomplished in the person of His Son, Jesus:

> Therefore, now that we have been justified through faith, let us continue at peace with God through our Lord, Jesus Christ, through whom we have been allowed to enter the sphere of God's grace, where we now stand. Let us exult in the hope of the divine splendour that is to be ours . . . because God's love has flooded our inmost heart through the Holy Spirit He has given us. (Rom. 5.1–5)

Just think about this language for a moment and consider the quite staggering claim it is making. 'We have been allowed to enter the sphere of God's grace, where we now stand.' 'God's love has flooded our inmost heart through the Holy Spirit He has given us.' St Paul was no mere theorist. He was a passionate announcer of a real event that he was trying to make all realize and his words were urgent indicators of this event as a reality shared by all. His great conviction is, that the central reality of our Christian faith is the sending of the Spirit of Jesus; indeed our faith is a living faith precisely because the living Spirit of God dwells within us, giving new life to our mortal bodies.

The all-important aim in Christian meditation is to allow God's mysterious and silent presence within us to become more and more not only *a* reality, but *the* reality in our lives; to let it become that reality which gives meaning, shape and purpose to everything we do, to everything we are.

Meditation is a learning process. It is a process of learning to pay attention, to concentrate, to attend. W. H. Auden made the point well when he said that schools were places that should be teaching the spirit of prayer in a secular context. This they would do, he maintained, by teaching people how to concentrate fully and exclusively on whatever was before them, be it poem, picture, maths problem, or leaf under a microscope, and to concentrate on these for their own sake. By the 'spirit of prayer', he meant selfless attention. (W. H. Auden, 'A Certain World', *A Commonplace Book*, Viking Press, New York, 1970, p. 306).

In learning to meditate, then, we must pay attention firstly to ourselves. We must become fully aware of who we are. If we can really apprehend for a moment the truth that we are created by God, we can begin to sense something of our own potentiality. We have a divine origin. God is our Creator. And in the Christian vision we know that God is not only a once-for-all Creator who creates us and then leaves us to ourselves, but He is also equally our loving Father. This is the truth about ourselves that we commemorate, pay full attention to in meditation. It is only because we forget this fundamental truth that we treat ourselves so trivially for so much of the time, our lives slipping through our fingers while we are either too busy or too bored to remember who we are. The reason why we can become so trivial, and why we can find ourselves and our lives so boring, is simply that we do not pay enough attention to our divine origin, our divine redemption by Jesus who has redeemed us from both triviality and boredom. Nor do we pay attention to our own holiness as temples of the Holy Spirit.

Meditation is the process in which we take time to allow ourselves to become aware of our infinite potential in the context of the Christ-event. As St Paul puts it in Chapter 8 of Romans: 'And those whom He called, He has justified, and to those whom He justified, He has also given His splendour' (Rom. 8.30).

In meditation we open ourselves up to this splendour. Put another way, this means that in meditation we discover both who we are and why we are. In meditation we are not running away from ourselves, we are finding ourselves; we are not rejecting

4

ourselves, we are affirming ourselves. St Augustine put this very succinctly and very beautifully when he said: 'Human beings must first be restored to themselves that, making in themselves as it were a stepping-stone, they may rise thence and be borne up to God' (*Retractions* 1 (viii) 3, Migne PL XXXII).

It is probable that most of us will be familiar with all that I have written so far. We know that God is our Creator. We know that Jesus is our Redeemer. We know too that Jesus has sent His Spirit to dwell within us, and we have some sort of idea about our eternal destiny. But the great weakness of most Christians is, that although they know these truths on the level of theological theory, the truths do not really live in their hearts. In other words, these truths that are thought are not realized. We know them as propositions propounded by the Church, by theologians, by preachers from pulpits, or in magazines, but we have not realized them as the grounding truths of our lives, as the sure basis which gives us conviction and authority.

There is nothing essentially new or modern therefore about the Christian context of meditation. Its aim is to turn to our own nature with total concentration, to experience our own creation first-hand and, above all, to turn to and experience the living Spirit of God dwelling in our hearts. The life of that Spirit within us is indestructible and eternal and, in this sense, the truths that make the Christian context of meditation are always new and permanently modern.

In meditation we do not seek to think about God nor do we seek to think about His Son, Jesus, nor do we seek to think about the Holy Spirit. We are trying rather to do something immeasurably greater. By turning aside from everything that is passing, everything that is contingent, we seek not just to think about God, but to be with God, to experience God as the ground of our being. It is one thing to know that Jesus is the Revelation of the Father, that Jesus is our Way to the Father, but quite another

5

to experience the presence of Jesus within us, to experience the real power of His Spirit within us and, in that experience, to be brought into the presence of my Father and your Father.

Many people today are finding that they have to face the fact that there is an all-important difference between thinking about these truths of the Christian faith and experiencing them, between believing them on hearsay and believing them from our own personal verification. Experiencing and verifying these truths is not just the work of specialists in prayer. St Paul's inspiring and exultant letters were not written to members of an enclosed religious Order, but to the ordinary butchers and bakers of Rome, Ephesus and Corinth.

These are truths that each one of us is called to know for himself, and in meditation we seek to know them.

Learning to be Silent

We now need to take a closer look at the sort of silence that is needed for meditation. Meditation is not the time for words, however beautifully and sincerely phrased. All our words are wholly ineffective when we come to enter into this deep and mysterious communion with God whose own Word within us is before and after all words. 'I am the Alpha and the Omega,' says the Lord.

In order to enter into this holy and mysterious communion with the Word of God dwelling within us, we must first have the courage to become more and more silent. In a deep creative silence we meet God in a way that transcends all our powers of intellect and language. We are all basically aware that we cannot apprehend God by thought. What the philosopher Alfred Whitehead said of human investigation of time could apply equally to human thought of God. He wrote: 'It is impossible to meditate on time and the mystery of the creative passage of nature without an

overwhelming emotion at the limitations of human intelligence'
(Cf. G. H. Whitrow, *The Nature of Time*, Penguin, 1975, p. 144).

The experience of this 'overwhelming emotion' at our own
limitations leads us into a silence where we have to listen, to
concentrate, to attend rather than to think. The mystery of our
relationship with God is one that embraces such a vast canvas
that only by developing our capacity for awe-filled and reverential silence will we ever be able to appreciate even a fraction of its
wonder. We know that God is intimately with us and also infinitely beyond us. It is only through deep and liberating silence
that we can reconcile the polarities of this mysterious paradox.
And the liberation that we experience in silent prayer is precisely liberation from the inevitably distorting effects of language
when we begin to experience God's intimate and transcendent
dominion within us. Anyone who has experienced this liberating work of the Spirit knows exactly what St Paul means when he
writes to the Romans in Chapter 8: 'It follows, my friends, that
our lower nature has no claim upon us; we are not obliged to live
on that level' (Rom. 8.12).

He puts it with the same wonderful confidence in his letter to
the Colossians in Chapter 1: 'He rescued us from the domain of
darkness and brought us away into the kingdom of His dear Son'
(Col. 1.13).

It is because this kingdom is established and is present within
us that we can be made free of the limitations of language and
thought.

Our attempt to achieve this silence my be difficult. It will
almost certainly be prolonged. It is not just a matter of keeping
our tongues still but much more of achieving a state of alert stillness in our mind and heart, which is not a state of consciousness
familiar to most Westerners. We tend either to be alert or relaxed;
rarely are the two states combined in most of us. But in meditation we come to experience ourselves as at one and the same time

totally relaxed and totally alert. This stillness is not the stillness of sleep but rather of totally awakened concentration.

If you look at a watchmaker about to perform some deft movement with a fine pair of tweezers, you will notice how still and poised he is as he scrutinizes the inside of the watch through his eyeglass. His stillness, however, is one of complete concentration, serious absorption in what he is doing. Similarly in meditation our stillness is not a state of mere passivity but a state of full openness, full wakefulness to the wonder of our own being, full openness to the wonder of God, the author and the sustainer of our being, and a full awareness that we are at one with God.

Here are some very simple and practical hints. To meditate well you should adopt a comfortable sitting posture; it must be comfortable and relaxed, but not sloppy. The back should be as straight as possible with the spine in an upright position. Those who possess a fair degree of suppleness and agility may sit on the floor in a cross-legged position. If you sit in a chair, make sure it is one that is upright with comfortable arm-rests. Your breathing should be calm and regular. Allow every muscle in your body to relax. And then, put the mind in tune with the body. The interior dispositions you need are a calm mind and a peaceful spirit, and it is here that the challenge of meditation lies. It is easy enough to sit still, and we must learn to sit quite still, but the real task of meditation is to achieve the harmony of body, mind and spirit. This is what we mean when we talk about the peace of God, a peace that passes all understanding.

The Indian mystic Sri Ramakrishna, who lived in Bengal in the nineteenth century, used to describe the mind as a mighty tree filled with monkeys, all swinging from branch to branch and all in an incessant riot of chatter and movement. When we begin to meditate we recognize that as a wonderfully apt description of the constant whirl going on in our mind. Prayer is not a matter of adding to this confusion by trying to shout it down and covering it with another lot of chatter. The task of meditation is to bring all of this mobile and distracted mind to stillness, silence and concentration, to bring it, that is, into its proper service. This is the aim given us by the psalmist: 'Be still and know that I am God.' To achieve this aim we use a very simple device. It is one that St Benedict drew to the attention of his monks as long ago as the sixth century by directing them to read the *Conferences* of John Cassian (*Rule of St Benedict* 42.6, 13; 73.14).

Cassian recommended anyone who wanted to learn to pray, and to pray continually, to take a single short verse and just to repeat this verse over and over again. In his tenth *Conference*, he urges this method of simple and constant repetition as the best way of casting out all distractions and monkey chatter from our mind, in order that it might rest in God (Cassian, *Conference* 10.10).

When I read Cassian on this, I am immediately reminded of the prayer that Jesus approved of when He tells us of the sinner who stood at the back of the temple and prayed in the single phrase: 'Lord, be merciful to me a sinner, Lord, be merciful to me a sinner.' He went home 'justified', Jesus tells us, whereas the Pharisee who stood at the front of the temple in loud eloquent prayer did not (Luke 18.9–14). The whole of the teaching of Cassian on prayer is based on the Gospels: 'In your prayers do not go on babbling like the heathen, who imagine that the more they say, the more likely they are to be heard. Do not imitate them. Your Father knows what your needs are before you ask Him' (Matt. 6.7–8).

As I have suggested, prayer is not a matter of talking to God, but of listening to and being with God. It is this simple understanding of prayer that lies behind John Cassian's advice that if we want to pray, to listen, we must become quiet and still, by reciting a short verse over and over again. Cassian received this method as something which was an old, established tradition in his own day and it is an enduring universal tradition. A thousand years after Cassian, the English author of *The Cloud of Unknowing* recommends the repetition of a little word: 'We must pray in the height, depth, length and breadth of our spirit [he says], not in many words but in a little word' (*The Cloud of Unknowing*, ch. 39).

As this idea may be a novel one, and indeed even sound rather strange, let me repeat the basic technique of meditation. Sit down comfortably, relax. Make sure you are sitting upright. Breathe calmly and regularly. Close your eyes and then in your mind begin to repeat the word that you have chosen as your meditation word.

The name for this prayer-word, called '*formula*' in Latin, is in the Eastern tradition *mantra*. So from now on I will use the phrase 'saying the mantra'. Choosing your word or mantra is of some importance. Ideally, again, you should choose your mantra in consultation with your teacher. But there are various mantras which are possible for a beginner. If you have no teacher to help you, then you should choose a word that has been allowed over the centuries by our Christian tradition. Some of these words were first taken over as mantras for Christian meditation by the Church in its earliest days. One of these is the word 'maranatha'. This is the mantra I recommend to most beginners, the Aramaic word 'maranatha' which means, 'Come Lord. Come Lord Jesus.'

It is the word that St Paul uses to end his first letter to the Corinthians (1 Cor. 16.22), and the word with which St John ends the book of Revelation (Rev. 22.20). It also has a place in some of the earliest Christian liturgies (*Didache* 10.6). I prefer the Aramaic form because it has no associations for most of us and it helps us into a meditation that will be quite free of all images. The name Jesus would be another possibility as a mantra, and so would the word that Jesus Himself used in His prayer, namely, 'Abba'. This is again an Aramaic word which means 'Father'. The important thing to remember about your mantra is to choose it, if possible in consultation with a teacher, and then to keep to it. If you chop and change your mantra you are postponing your progress in meditation.

John Cassian speaks of the purpose of meditation as that of restricting the mind to the poverty of a single verse. A little later, he shows his full meaning in an illuminating phrase. He talks about becoming *'grandly poor'* (*Conference* 10.11). Meditation will certainly give you new insights into poverty. As you persevere with the mantra, you will begin to understand more and more deeply, out of your own experience, what Jesus meant when He said, 'Blessed are the poor in spirit' (Matt. 5.3). You will also learn in a very concrete way the meaning of faithfulness as you persevere in fidelity to the repetition of the mantra.

In meditation, then, we declare our own poverty. We renounce words, thoughts, imaginations and we do so by restricting the mind to the poverty of one word, and thus the process of meditation is simplicity itself. In order to experience its benefits, it is necessary to meditate twice a day and every day, without fail. Twenty minutes is the minimum time for meditation, twenty-five or thirty minutes is about the average time. It is also helpful to meditate regularly in the same place and also at the same time every day because this helps a creative rhythm in our life to grow, with meditation as a kind of pulse-beat sounding the rhythm. But when all is said and done, the most important thing to bear in mind about meditation is to remain faithfully repeating the mantra throughout the time you put aside for it, throughout the time of what the author of *The Cloud of Unknowing* called 'the time of the work' (*The Cloud of Unknowing*, ch. 4–7, 36–40).

The Power of the Mantra

All Christian prayer is basically the experience of being filled with the Spirit, and so, in any talking or thinking about prayer we should fix the spotlight firmly on the Spirit not ourselves. In Romans 8, Paul puts it this way: 'We do not even know how to pray, but through our inarticulate groans the Spirit Himself is pleading for us, and God who searches our inmost being knows what the Spirit means' (Rom. 8.26–27).

This experience of prayer, of being filled with the Spirit, increases our capacity for wonder and our capacity for understanding the transcendent potential of our own being. There is a sense in which we can say that before prayer our principal conviction about reality is of its limitations. We see everything in its transient dimension passing away from us. We feel ourselves caught in the Buddhist *samsara*, the unavoidable cycle of birth and death. But after prayer our principal conviction about ourselves and the whole creation is of the infinite capacity in everything to mediate the wonder and splendour of God.

A marvellous thing then happens. With this growing sense of wonder at God's power within us there comes an ever-deepening awareness of the harmony, the creative wholeness that we possess, and we begin to feel that we know ourselves for the first time. But the truly transcendent nature of this discovery is that we do not begin to appreciate our own personal harmony alone, but we begin to experience it as a new capacity for true empathy, a capacity to be at peace with others, and indeed at peace with the whole of creation.

In meditation our way forward to this growing awareness of the Spirit praying within us lies simply in our deepening fidelity to the saying of the mantra. It is the faithful repetition of our word that integrates our whole being. It does so because it brings

us to the silence, the concentration, the necessary level of consciousness that enable us to open our mind and heart to the work
of the love of God in the depth of our being.

To understand the process once more, begin by sitting down
comfortably and calmly and then start to say your mantra in the
silence of your mind: Maranatha, Ma-ra-na-tha. Repeat the word
calmly, serenely, and above all faithfully for the full time of your
meditation, that is for about twenty to thirty minutes. We begin
by saying the mantra in the mind. For modern Western people
who have so restricted ourselves to the mental modality, there is
no other way to begin. But as we progress with simple fidelity, the
mantra begins to sound not so much in our head but rather in
our heart. That is, it seems to become rooted in the very depths
of our being.

The spiritual masters of the Orthodox Church have always
emphasized the essential importance of what they call the 'prayer
of the heart'. They see the fundamental consequence of the fall
as the separation of mind and heart in the human person, and
indeed this sense of inner division pervades the whole Western
sense of self-understanding. The twentieth-century word for sin
is alienation. If we ponder the wide spectrum of meaning that
word has for us, the Marxist sense, the sense of powerlessness,
meaninglessness, self-estrangement, the failure to find adequate
norms for social or personal relationships, and if we ponder these
conceptions we have of ourselves, we will realize how deeply
divided we are. In the context of meditation all these many alienations resolve into that one basic division between mind and
heart. The mind is our organ for truth; the heart is our organ for
love. But they cannot work independently of each other without
filling us with a sense of failure, dishonesty, deep boredom or
frenetic evasion of ourselves through busyness.

The truly religious understanding of our humanity is not found
in terms of reward and punishment, but in terms of wholeness

and division. The supreme religious insight in the East and West is that all our alienations are resolved, and all our thinking and feeling powers united, in the heart. One of the *Upanishads* says that the mind must be kept in the heart (*Maitri Upanishad* 6.24). St Paul proclaims the same vision of the human person's unity when he gives love the supremacy over every other dimension and activity (1 Cor. 13.13). The saints of the Orthodox Church see the essential task of the Christian life as being to restore this unity to us with a mind and heart integrated through prayer. The mantra provides this integrating power. It is like a harmonic that we sound in the depths of our spirit, bringing us to an ever-deepening sense of our own wholeness and central harmony. It leads us to the source of this harmony, to our centre, rather as a radar bleep leads an aircraft home through thick fog. It also rearranges us, in the sense that it brings all our powers and faculties into line with each other just as a magnet drawn over iron filings pulls them into their proper force fields.

In starting to meditate, we have three preliminary aims. The first is simply to say the mantra for the full duration of the meditation. It will probably take some time to achieve this first stage and we will have to learn patience in the meantime. Meditating is an entirely natural process for all of us, for just as our physical growth takes place in its own natural rhythm, with variations for each individual, so does our prayer life develop quite naturally. We cannot force anything to happen but must simply say the mantra without haste, or expectation.

The second aim is to say the mantra throughout the meditation without interruption, while remaining quite calm in the face of all distractions. In this phase, the mantra resembles a plough that continues resolutely across the rough field of our mind, undeflected by any obtrusion or disturbance.

And the third of these preliminary aims is to say the mantra for the entire time of the meditation, quite free of all distractions. The surface areas of the mind are now in tune with the deep peacefulness at the core of our being. The same harmonic sounds throughout our being. In this state we have passed beyond thought, beyond imagination, and beyond all images. We simply rest with the Reality, the realized presence of God Himself dwelling within our hearts.

As you read this, you may think that it is a very ambitious endeavour. But it is an endeavour we make in response to the invitation of Jesus to leave all things and to follow Him (Luke 9.23). Leaving all these thoughts and imaginations, we seek to follow Him in the purity of our heart. Meditation in this sense is a purifying process. In Blake's phrase: 'If the doors of perception were cleansed, everything will appear to man as it is, infinite' (*A Memorable Fancy: The Ancient Tradition*). By means of the mantra we leave behind all passing images and learn to rest in the infinity of God Himself. St Paul urges us to do just this when he implores us in Romans 12:

> ... by God's mercy to offer your very selves to Him: a living sacrifice, dedicated and fit for His acceptance, the worship offered by mind and heart. Adapt yourselves no longer to the pattern of this present world, but let your minds be remade and your whole nature thus transformed. (Rom. 12.1–2)

This transformation of our nature is put before us as a real and an immediate possibility. It is also the essential Christian experience, the experience of being born again in the Holy Spirit, being born again when we realize the power of the living Spirit of God within us. By becoming aware of its presence within us we, as it were, set it free to work freely within us to transform us. The mantra is simply the device which leads us to this central Christian experience, leading us to know from our own experience that God's love has flooded our inmost heart through the Holy Spirit He has given us (Rom. 5.5).

It is so easy for a modern Christian to read words like those of St Paul with veiled hearts and closed minds, never knowing for himself what Paul so exultantly knew from within and tried to communicate to us. We may accept it notionally. We may even preach it. But if we lack authority and confidence and courage, it is because we have not ourselves experienced its immediate and enduring reality. 'Know it', Paul tells us, 'though it is beyond knowledge' (Eph. 3.18). We have to prepare our hearts to receive the wonderful message of the gospel in all its fullness. And until we have expanded our consciousness, we will be incapable of taking in anything of the grand scale of the message of our redemption, and we will be incapable too of knowing what the traditional religious language we use really means. Until an expansion of our consciousness takes place our minds and hearts will be too limited, too absorbed in day-to-day trivia. Meditation is precisely the way we need to follow in order to expand our hearts, broaden our vision and, as Blake said, 'cleanse the doors of our perception'.

This should give you some idea of the perspective which regular meditation can open up. There are, of course, stages we pass through en route to the full realization of the Kingdom of God within us. But we should not waste time and energy worrying about what stage we have reached. 'Unless you become like little children, you cannot enter the Kingdom of Heaven' (Mark 10.15). What we must do is to begin to meditate, to begin to open ourselves up to the love of God and its power. To do this, all we need to do is to begin to say the mantra, lovingly and in a deep spirit of faith.

The stages of our progress in meditation will come about in their own time. God's own time. We in fact only hinder this progression by becoming too self-conscious about our stage of development. This is where a teacher is of immense help for keeping you on a straight course. But basically your teacher has only one instruction to give you and that is: to say your mantra. More than this is simply encouragement and comfort until the mantra is rooted in your consciousness. The path of enlightenment is one we tread for ourselves. Each person wins wisdom for himself. The teacher is there to keep you steadily going forward. The word 'guru' itself, dispeller of darkness, means the one who is steady.

The greatest temptation of all is to complicate ourselves. 'Unless you become like little children . . .' Meditation simplifies us, simplifies us to the point where we can receive the fullness of truth and the fullness of love. It prepares us and enables us to listen with childlike attention to the Spirit of Jesus within us. As we persevere in meditation, we enter ever more deeply into relationship with this Spirit, with God who is love dwelling in our hearts, enlightening us and vitalizing us.

The Fullness of Life

When people look at meditation for the first time from outside, they often mistake it for just another form of fashionable egocentric introversion. It often appears to the outsider that meditators go into themselves so much, so often, that they are rather betraying a deep-rooted and unhealthy narcissism. That it should appear like this is really quite understandable, because, as we have seen in St Augustine's phrase, we must first be 'restored to ourselves that we might rise thence to God'. In meditating we do affirm our faith in the gift of our own creation. We recognize the wonder of our own being, and we are prepared to spend time and to persevere in coming to terms with it. For Jesus has told us that His mission was to bring us fullness of life: 'I have come that people may have life, and may have it in all its fullness' (John 10.10). In making this declaration. He assures us in the same Gospel of St John that it is He Himself who is the Way to this fullness. He tells us that He is the Light of the world and, 'no follower of mine shall wander in the dark; he shall have the light of life' (John 8.12). In beginning to meditate we are declaring a courageous acceptance of this invitation of Jesus and we enter into our meditation on each occasion as the twin process of vitalization and enlightenment.

What emerges so triumphantly from the teaching of Jesus, and from the understanding of that teaching by the early Church, is that this Life and this Light are quite literally to be found within each of us. St Paul writes, not to specialists, nor to a group of Carthusians or Carmelites, but to the ordinary citizens of Rome: 'Moreover, if the Spirit of Him who raised Jesus from the dead dwells within you, then the God who raised Christ Jesus from the dead will also give new life to your mortal bodies through His indwelling spirit' (Rom. 8.11).

Meditation summons us to open our hearts to this light and to this life by the very simple expedient of paying attention; that is, paying attention to their presence within us. We pay attention to our own true nature, and by becoming fully conscious of the union of our nature with Christ, we become fully ourselves. By becoming fully ourselves we enter the fullness of life Jesus has brought us. We come to appreciate, in the reverent silence of our prayer, that we are infinitely holy as temples of God's own Spirit. We learn to remember who we are, and that our vocation is to look upon and contemplate the Godhead itself and thus to be ourselves divinized. As the third Eucharistic Prayer expresses it: 'On that day we shall see You our God as You are and we shall become like You.' The great masters of prayer in the Christian tradition have understood prayer in this way as a discovery of self that takes us far beyond narrow self-consciousness, a discovery made by making of ourselves a stepping-stone. The twelfth-century Scot, Richard of St Victor, expresses it so clearly and simply:

The rational soul finds in itself the chief and principal mirror for seeing God. Let him who desires to see God wipe his mirror and cleanse his heart. When the mirror has been cleansed and examined a long time carefully, a brightness of the divine light begins to shine through to him and a great beam of illumination not known hitherto appears before our eyes. (Richard of St Victor, *Selected Writings on Contemplation*, ed. Kirchberger, Faber & Faber, 1957, p. 102)

Saying the mantra is just this process of polishing the mirror, the mirror within us, so that our heart becomes fully open to the work of God's love for us, fully reflecting the light of that love. We must understand very clearly that the first step in this process is to set our own house in order. Meditation is thus a process of self-discovery. By faithfulness to the twice-daily meditation we find that in the Christian tradition self-discovery and self-affirmation are the realizations of our own true grandeur and true splendour in Christ. St Catherine of Genoa put it in this way: 'My me is God nor do I know my selfhood save in Him' (cf. E. Underhill, *The Mystics of the Church*, James Clarke, 1975, p. 51). In the Indian tradition the same understanding finds expression in the assertion that our first task is the discovery of our own true inner self, the Atman, which is the means of becoming aware of union with the ultimate universal self, which is Brahman, which is God.

Similarly, in the Christian perspective, we see the great task of prayer as the realization of our intimate union with God, our Father, through Christ in the Spirit. St Gregory wrote of St Benedict that 'he dwelt within himself always in the presence of his Creator and not allowing his eyes to gaze on distractions' (*Dialogues*, Book II, ch. 3). There is something extraordinarily attractive about the description. It reveals an understanding of the Father of Western Monasticism as above all a man of prayer. 'He dwelt within himself.' That tells us that, in Gregory's view,

Benedict had realized a wholeness and harmony that had dispelled all false ideas, all illusions about himself, illusions which are necessarily outside of ourselves.

The task we have is to find our way back to our creative centre where wholeness and harmony are realized, to dwell within ourselves, leaving behind all the false images of ourselves such as what we think we are or what we think we might have been, because these have an unreal existence outside of us. Remaining within ourselves in this sense of illusion-shattering honesty and simplicity, leads us to remain always in the presence of our Creator. This is where the mantra is a device of such importance. As we learn to root it in our consciousness, the mantra becomes like a key that opens the door to the secret chamber of our heart. At first, in the set times of our meditation, both morning and evening, saying the mantra is work. We have to learn to become thoroughly familiar with it. But as we progress, as we begin to sound it and to listen to it, then, each and every time we recite it, we enter into and remain in our heart. Thus, by merely calling the mantra to mind at other times of the day, we enter straight away into the presence of the Creator who dwells within us: 'I am with you always,' says the Lord (Matt. 28.20).

Learning to pray is learning to live as fully as possible in the present moment. In meditation we seek to enter as fully as we can into the now, and in entering into the now to live as fully as possible with the now-risen and ever-loving Lord Jesus. To be thus fully committed to the present moment is to find ourselves, to enter into ourselves, to dwell within ourselves; and this we do by renouncing thought and image. In meditation we are not thinking about the past, neither our own past nor anyone else's, nor are we thinking about the future, our own nor anyone else's. In meditation we are wholly inserted into the present, and there we live to the fullness of our capability, our consciousness expanding as we entertain the Lord of Life. The experience of this being wholly conscious is an experience of unity and simplicity.

First of all, we are conscious of our own wholeness and unity, and as we stay in this state of consciousness we experience a growing awareness of our unity with all persons, with all creation, with our Creator. As we rest in this state of heightened consciousness we begin to understand more and more of what St Paul meant when he wrote such words as these to the Ephesians: 'So may you attain to fullness of being, the very fullness of God' (Eph. 3.19). We begin to understand that to be, is to be here and now.

This is a journey we have to make, a pilgrimage which is a pilgrimage to our own heart. It is a pilgrimage that requires a certain amount of nerve. As Eliot put it in *The Four Quartets*: 'Human kind cannot bear very much reality' (from 'Burnt Norton I', *The Four Quartets*, Faber & Faber, 1979). Meditation is our way of leaving behind all the illusions about ourselves, about others, and about God, which we have either created for ourselves or received from the past.

As we advance into the silence we begin to experience the true meaning of the words of Jesus: 'Whoever would find their life must first lose it.' And again, 'Anyone who wishes to be a follower of mine, must leave self behind' (Mark 9.34–36). It requires nerve to become really quiet. To learn just to say the mantra and turn away from all thought requires courage. But as we persevere we discover that the poverty of the mantra leads us to a really radical simplicity that makes this courage possible, for we are capable of greater courage than we usually believe of ourselves. But meditation is the prayer of faith, because we have to leave ourselves behind before the Other appears and with no pre-packaged guarantee that God will appear. The essence of poverty consists in this risk of annihilation. This is the leap of faith from ourselves to the Other. This is the risk involved in all loving.

There comes a delicate moment in our progress when we begin to understand the totality of the commitment involved in self-surrendering prayer, when we see the total poverty involved in the mantra. This is a moment again where the help of a teacher could be critical. But in essence the invitation to meditate is a simple one. We meditate simply to prepare ourselves to receive that fullness and life and light for which we were created.

Meditation:
The Christian Experience

THE SELF

1 Corinthians 2.14

'Know then, thyself; presume not God to scan. The proper study of mankind is man.' When Alexander Pope wrote those lines in his *Essay on Man* he enjoyed a far greater trust in human beings' essential reasonableness than prevails today, and his confidence in humanity was something more than a merely rational humanism. It assumed a common faith in essential human goodness, in the fundamentally positive meaning of life and a common sense of the presence of an order in human affairs and of a harmony in the unfolding energies of the cosmos. Our confidence in ourselves today is much less secure. We are more likely to see ourselves as having unleashed powers we can no longer control and of having exploited the earth's natural resources so wantonly that we are in danger of exhausting them by the time our grandchildren have reached maturity.

But perhaps the primary cause of our confusion and alienation is that we have lost the support of a common faith in humanity's essential goodness, reasonableness and inner integrity, indeed of any common faith at all. Where we find our community, our community of thought, and of feeling (and find it or concoct it we must) is much more likely to be in self-recrimination and prophecies of doom; or in protest, which is usually a protestation against and seldom a witness for. Now this is perhaps a part of our fallen nature that we have to live with, namely, that much common sympathy between people is built upon this negative base of sharing the same fears and the same prejudices. But it is possible to enjoy a deeper, more positive unity which is rooted in a common awareness of the potential of the human spirit rather than the limitations of human life. It is the specifically Christian task to sink the roots of this awareness deep into modern self-understanding and our sense of the world.

If our Christianity is more than just another ideology on a comparative religion programme, if it is a life we receive and mediate, we have to ask ourselves a question: 'Why is it that the power of this risen life of Jesus is not being mediated through us to transform the negative energies of modern self-rejection into the positive awareness of the depth and richness of our own spirit?'

In the ancient myth of the Fisher King, the land has been blighted by a curse that has frozen all the waters and turned the earth to stone. No power in the land can lift the curse and the king sits silently fishing through a hole in the ice, despondent, waiting. One day a stranger approaches and asks the king the redemptive question. Immediately the waters thaw and the earth softens.

Religious people have so often pretended to have all the answers. They have seen their mission as being to persuade, to enforce, to level differences and perhaps even to impose uniformity. There is really something of the Grand Inquisitor in most religious people. But when religion begins to bully or to insinuate, it has become unspiritual because the first gift of the Spirit, creatively moving in human nature, is freedom and frankness; in biblical language, liberty and truth. The modern Christian mission is to resensitize our contemporaries to the presence of a spirit within themselves. We are not teachers in the sense that we are providing answers that we have looked up in the back of a book. We are truly teachers when, having found our own spirit, we can inspire others to accept the responsibility of their own being, to undergo the challenge of their own innate longing for the Absolute, to find their own spirit.

To be able to do this work of inspiration, it is not enough to be courageous, though courage is needed. Moses cried to God in fear, 'But they will never believe me; they will say, "the Lord did not appear to you"' (Exod. 4.1). Nor is it enough to be eloquent, though eloquence will be given. No human quality can of itself undertake to ask the redemptive question. Whenever we discover ourselves acting as an instrument of the Word, it is when we know ourselves directed by the Spirit. And to know this is to have seen our own spirit; it is to have glimpsed the depths of our own spirit and know that our spirit is of God.

To know this, though as St Paul said, it is beyond knowledge, is to be born over again in Spirit, and to undergo the seminal Christian experience which ignited the early Church and burst into the preaching of St Paul and of the saints down the ages. It is the experience that begins in the silent encounter within ourselves. For it, only one condition needs to be fulfilled, namely, that we subject everything else to it: possessions, possessiveness, desire and honour, body and mind. We renounce everything in order to attain to that complete simplicity that demands not less than everything, which opens our eyes to the living presence of the loving Lord Jesus within us and His Spirit ever returning into communion with the Father. 'Whoever does not possess the Spirit of Christ, is no Christian' (Rom. 8.9), St Paul tells us. The redemptive question that Christians should ask to set their contemporaries free rises from the depths of their experience of spirit and inspires the unspiritual to discover those same depths within themselves. We can only talk though of what we have seen. The Gospel of John reminds us that it is only spirit that can give birth to spirit (John 3.6).

Few generations have been so introverted and self-analytical as our own, and yet modern self-analysis can be notoriously unproductive. The reason for this, as I have been suggesting, is that it has been radically unspiritual; that is, it has not been conducted in the light of the Spirit, it has not taken account of that real and fundamental dimension of our nature. Without spirit there is no productivity, no creativity, no possibility of growth. The Christian's duty is to point this out, and to be able to do so with the authority of one who really knows what spirit is, but only because we know our own spirit and that infinite expansion of our spirit that takes place when it responds to the presence of the Spirit of God, from whom it derives its being.

Such a Christian possesses power, the power of the Risen Lord, and it is a power that consists in the liberation of spirit that is achieved through the cycle of death and resurrection, through our participation in the dying and rising of Jesus. What dies as we persevere in opening ourselves to the Spirit is our narrow limited ego and all the petty concerns and ambitions with which it boards over the shaft of our being; what dies is the fear we experience as we see the light emerging from this shaft; what dies is everything that obstructs us from realizing life, life in all its fullness. This discovery of our own spirit, our real self, is an experience that consists of an indescribable joy, the joy of liberation. But the loss of self which makes it possible, the erosion and the shedding of long familiar illusions require those qualities which have so important a place in St Paul's teaching: boldness, courage, faith, commitment and perseverance. It is these qualities, mundane rather than heroic, which enable us to persevere in the daily commitment to the pilgrimage, the fidelity to the twice-daily meditation and the 'grand poverty' to which the mantra leads us. These are not home-grown qualities, they are given to us by love, gifts from the Spirit to lead us to God, to deeper love. There is no way to truth or to the Spirit that is not the way of love. God is love.

In discovering our own spirit, we are led to our creative centre whence our essence is being emanated and renewed by the loving overflow of the life of the Trinity. We find our own spirit fully only in the light of the One Spirit, just as we are sustained and expanded by our love for each other and know ourselves when we allow ourselves to be known by them. To see ourselves, we must look at another, for the way to selfhood is the way of otherness.

It is not enough to concur with these statements merely as conceptual realities. Our rational process can, of course, by the guidance of the Spirit itself, begin the process of rebirth in Spirit. It can lead us to uncover and expand our own spirit, but no merely conceptual expression is in itself the experience of our true self. No intellectual self-analysis can substitute for real self-knowledge in the ground of our being. There are many words and terms from many traditions in which we can try to express the purpose of meditation, of prayer. Here I am suggesting only this preliminary purpose, that in the silence of our meditation, in our attentiveness to the Other, in our patient waiting, we find our own spirit.

The fruit of this discovery is very rich. We know then that we share in the nature of God, that we are called ever deeper into the joyous depths of God's own self-communion, and this is no peripheral purpose of the Christian life. In fact, if it is Christian and if it is alive, our life must place this at the very centre of all we do and aim to do. 'Our whole business in this life', said St Augustine, 'is to restore to health the eye of the heart whereby God may be seen' (*Serm. de Script, N.T.*, 88 v. 5). This eye is our spirit. Our first task, in the realization of our own vocation and in the expansion of the kingdom among our contemporaries, is to find our own spirit because this is our life-line with the Spirit of God. In doing so, we come to realize that we participate in the divine progression and that we share the dynamic essence of God's still point: harmony, light, joy and love.

To fulfil this destiny we are called to transcendence, to that continuous state of liberty and perpetual renewal, that complete passing into the other. In our meditation we begin to enter this state by our renunciation of words, images, thoughts and even self-consciousness, everything which is in itself contingent, ephemeral, tangential. In meditation we must have the courage to attend solely to the Absolute, the abiding and the central. To find our own spirit, we must be silent and allow our spirit to emerge from the darkness to which it has been banished. To transcend we must be still. The stillness is our pilgrimage and the way of the pilgrim is the mantra.

THE SON

2 Corinthians 5.17

'It is better to be silent and real than to talk and be unreal,' wrote St Ignatius of Antioch in the first century (Eph. ch. 15), and our contemporary situation must surely bear this out. Authority, conviction, personal verification, which are the indispensable qualities of the Christian witness are not to be found in books, in discussions or on cassettes, but rather in an encounter with ourselves in the silence of our own spirit.

If modern people have lost their experience of spirit, pneuma or essence in which their own irreducible and absolute being consists, it is because we have lost our experience of and capacity for silence. There are few statements about the spiritual reality which can claim a universal agreement. But this one has received the same formulation in almost all traditions, namely, that it is only in accepting silence that we can come to know our own spirit, and only in abandonment to an infinite depth of silence that we can be revealed to the source of our spirit in which multiplicity and division disappear. People today are often deeply threatened by silence as what Eliot called, 'the growing terror of nothing to think about' ('East Coker III', *The Four Quartets*), and everyone has to face this fear when they begin to meditate.

First, we must confront with some shame the chaotic din of a mind ravaged by so much exposure to trivia and distraction. Persevering through this in fidelity to the mantra, we then encounter a darker level of consciousness, of repressed fears and anxieties. The radical simplicity of the mantra clears this too. But our first inclination is always to retreat from the dawn of self-knowledge and, as Walter Hilton very graphically expressed it, 'this is not surprising, for if a man came home to his house and found nothing but a smoking fire and a nagging wife, he would quickly run out again' (*The Scale of Perfection*, see Bibliography).

In entering upon these first two levels, of surface distractions and subconscious anxiety, we risk being bruised. But in entering into the next, into our own silence, we risk everything, for we risk our very being: 'So I said to my soul, "Be still."' The stillness of mind and body to which the mantra guides us is a preparation for entering this silence, and for our progression through the spheres of silence to see with wonder the light of our own spirit, and to know that light as something beyond our spirit and yet the source of it. This is a pilgrimage through our spheres of silence that we undertake in faith, putting our entire trust in what is only a dim apprehension of the authentic, the real, yet confident in doing so because it is authentic.

In saying the mantra, we lay down our life for the sake of Him we have not yet seen (1 Pet. 1.8). Blessed are they who believe and act on their belief though they have not yet seen. In saying the mantra we are plunged into a silence that explores our infinite poverty of mind and spirit, revealing our absolute dependence on another. We are led from depth to depth of purifying simplification until, having contacted the very ground of our being, we find the life we laid down and the self we surrendered in the Other.

St Paul claimed to carry the dying of Christ within himself and it was because of the authenticity of that perception that his witness to Christ was radiant with risen life (2 Cor. 4.10). It is precisely in this dying of Jesus that we all participate. St Luke's Gospel emphasizes that Jesus called upon all to renounce self and to take up their cross daily (Luke 9.23). To that call we respond when we meditate every day. We mislead ourselves and others if we try to play down the extremity of the Christian vocation and the total demand it makes. If we have been directed by the Spirit to undertake the pilgrimage, and every Christian is chosen to do so, then it must be with the mature understanding of what is at stake. As we enter the silence within us, having allowed ourselves to become aware of its presence in the first place, we are entering a void in which we are unmade. We cannot remain the person we were or thought we were. But we are, in fact, not being destroyed but awakened to the eternally fresh source of our being. We become aware that we are being created, that we are springing from the Creator's hand and returning to God in love.

In the silence, we are being prepared for this awakening which is an encounter with the fullness and the splendour of Jesus in that fully awakened state to which the Resurrection led Him, because no one comes to the Father of all except through the Son in whom all creation comes into being. But even if we know intellectually that this is the purpose of the silence, at the time our actual experience is of the void. In the beginning, we know reduction not expansion, a shedding of qualities and a contraction to the point of pure being in pure poverty of spirit, a cataclysmic simplicity.

In Christian understanding we all carry this dying within us as we go about our daily routine, not in a self-dramatizing or self-obsessed way, but with a joyful awareness that more and more deeply suffuses our whole being, that the degree to which we die to ourselves in this void is the degree to which we are revivified in the transcendent life of Jesus who is completely free. 'Though our outward humanity is in decay, yet day by day we are inwardly renewed' (2 Cor. 4.16). Within the structure of our daily life, this inward renewal of which St Paul speaks is the purpose and fruit of our twice-daily meditation. We are literally made new in the fact of entering into the ever-deeper centres of being, and of knowing ever more fully the harmony of all our qualities and energies in that ultimate centre of our being which is the centre and source of all being, the centre of the Trinitarian love. 'When anyone is united to Christ', Paul wrote to the Corinthians, 'there is a new world' (2 Cor. 5.17).

As Christians who enter into the cycle of death and resurrection more thoroughly, we become more aware of its universal truth, that it is the model of all being. We begin to appreciate what Mystery is. In order to become fully opened to the force of this universal cycle, we need to understand that it is completed at every level of every life, and in all of the countless ways in which we can examine or apprehend the meaning of our own life. It is, for example, the cycle upon which each half-hour of meditation is based, a death to the possessiveness and triviality occupying our ego and a rising to the liberty and significance that dawn when we find ourselves by looking fully at the Other. It is, too, the cycle upon which a whole lifetime of prayer can be seen on a large scale. We are dying and rising to new life every day as we participate in the evolution of God's plan for each of His creatures.

Yet it is also true that there is only one death and one rising, that which Jesus underwent for all creation. The Word proceeds from silence and it returns to the unfathomable silence and limitless love of the Father, the cycle of issuing and return upon which creation exists at every moment, could it but see this with a pure heart. But the Word does not return under the same conditions. By the Word's self-revelation in the depths of human being, which are the depths of God, the Word fulfils the Father's purpose, the source from whose silence the Word and, in it, creation proceed. It is the purpose for our being of which we have read a thousand times in Paul's words to the Ephesians and yet can never fully fathom:

> In Christ He chose us before the world was founded, to be dedicated, to be without blemish in his sight, to be full of love; and He destined us, such was His will and pleasure, to be accepted as His sons through Jesus Christ, in order that the glory of His gracious gift, so graciously bestowed upon us in His Beloved might redound to His praise. (Eph. 1.4–6)

It is a stupefying claim that our meaning is somehow involved in the meaning of God, and we need to have the courage that only utter simplicity affords in order to accept it. No egoism or complexity can awaken to this revelation: 'Unless you become like little children, you cannot enter the kingdom of Heaven.' We know that this claim is authentic because of our communion with the Word, the Son. All things and all beings return to the Father through the Son and of the Son, St John tells us that:

32

'Through Him all things came to be; no single thing was created without Him' (John 1.3). So just as He is the prime and ultimate expression of the Father, Jesus is also the hinge upon which the universe and all being swings back to the Father, its source. It is through our incorporation in the body of Christ in this swing-back to the Father that we are destined to be accepted as children of God.

In its essential significance, the aim of meditation is just this: the realization of our total incorporation in Jesus Christ, in the cycle of His utterance by, and return to, the Father. The qualities we need in this fundamental encounter between ourselves and the ground of our being are attentiveness and receptivity. In order to realize our complete incorporation with the Word, we have not only to listen to its silence, the silence within us, but also to allow the cycle of its life to be completed in us and to lead us into the depth of its silence. There in the silence of the Word we share His experience of hearing Himself eternally spoken by the Father.

This is why the life of Jesus is of such meaning and why Scripture's record of His life is of such value. The experience of Jesus of Nazareth in awakening to Himself, entering the spheres of silence within Himself, finding His own Spirit and the source of His Spirit, this experience is the experience of every person reborn in spirit. And it is, within the unimaginable design of the Father, the self-same experience. The wonder of creation is found, not in a succession of awakenings, but in the single all-inclusive awakening of Jesus, the Son, to the Father.

Our language is wholly inadequate and our thought too self-conscious to reflect the simplicity and actuality of this cycle of dying and rising. But it is not language or thought we need. We need only to become aware of the mystery within us, the silence in which we see our own spirit. Our path into this silence is the one little word of the mantra.

33

THE SPIRIT

1 Corinthians 6.19

The gospel of Jesus is different from every other programme of salvation precisely because it is personal. Jesus is a person, not a symbol or an archetype, and the way of salvation is our personal encounter with the person of Jesus in experiencing His all-redemptive love.

Because this is so, we know that we are called to become full persons, to become fully ourselves so that our encounter with Jesus may be fully personal, fully mature. There is, of course, nothing narrowly individualistic about growing into full person-hood. The human race is formed in such a way that the whole of humanity reaches its fulfilment in the individual, while the individual is realized only by knowing himself or herself incorporate in the whole. The communal corporate authority of the Church is derived from this truth, that is, from the depth to which her members have become persons, have actually experienced their own salvation in terms of the depth of the redemptive love of Jesus within them. We are all summoned to this experience here and now and it is our pre-eminent task to dispose ourselves for it. In our own day, this means transferring our conscious hopes for a renewal of the Church's relevance and effectiveness in the world from politics to prayer, from mind to heart, from committees to communities, from preaching to silence.

In fact, of course, the priority of prayer, of personal authentication, is a perennial one. 'To this end are celebrated the holy mysteries, to this end, the Word of God is preached, to this end, are the moral exhortations of the Church made,' wrote St Augustine (*Serm. de Script. N.T.,* 88 V5; vi, 6). And 'this end', as we have seen was 'to restore to health the eye of the heart whereby God may be seen'.

Every personal loving relationship has its source in the movement from lover to beloved, though it has its consummation in a wholly simple communion. If the Christian mystery depended upon the strength of our desire for God for its authenticity, it would be no more than a nostalgia for the numinous. But the actuality of our faith derives from the initiative that God has taken. 'The love I speak of', wrote St John, 'is not our love for God, but the love He showed to us in sending his Son' (1 John 4.10). As long as our faith is seen as comprising a movement from humanity to God, we can only remain self-centred, earthbound. But in apprehending it as the movement from God to us we discover ourselves caught up in that movement, in its own depths, self-transcending and returning to the Father through the Son. Another name for this movement is love.

The first step in personhood then is to allow ourselves to be loved. It was to facilitate this that the Holy Spirit was sent into the human heart, to touch it, to awaken it, to draw our mind into its redemptive light. The sending of the Spirit was a resurrection event and so continues as freshly today as it did 'late that Sunday evening', as St John tells us, when the disciples were together behind locked doors and Jesus came and breathed on them saying: 'Receive the Holy Spirit' (John 20.19–22). The natural lethargy and self-evasiveness of human nature, our reluctance to allow ourselves to be loved are, like the locked doors, no impediments to the Holy Spirit. The Spirit has been sent into the human heart, and it lives out the divine mystery there for as long as God sustains the person in being. In the heart of the utterly evil person, were there such a thing, the Holy Spirit would still be crying: 'Abba, Father' (Gal. 4.6), without ceasing.

In His resurrection and return to the Father, the human person who is Jesus, one of us, transcended every limitation of the human condition, the limitations of fear and ignorance, no less than those of time and space. He rose to a universal presence in the centre of all things. In human beings He achieved a living personal presence at the centre of our being which we know as the heart; and in us His presence is different from His presence in matter without consciousness. In us he lives as in a conscious being capable of expansion of consciousness, and of recognizing and responding on the level of the personal. The presence of Jesus within us, His Holy Spirit, calls out to us to become fully conscious of this level of our being. In the twinkling of an eye, we awaken to ourselves, to the Spirit dwelling in us, and thence to consciousness of the communion within God in which we are called to share. And so, we awaken not to a platonic aloneness but to a complete communion of all beings in Being itself.

We begin with a dim awareness of the stirring of the Spirit in our heart, the presence of Another by which we know ourselves. In awakening to its full reality, in listening to our heart, we awaken to the living proof of our faith justifying that first dim awareness, that first hope. And, as St Paul told the Romans: 'This proof is the ground of hope. Such a hope is no mockery because God's love has flooded our inmost heart through the Holy Spirit He has given us' (Rom. 5.4–5). The intoxication of Paul's language is the intoxication of his personal awakening to the Reality of the Spirit, to the experience of the joy released, pressed down and flowing over, which Jesus preached and communicates through His Spirit. It is the intoxication of prayer.

We have come to think of prayer largely as our movement to God, as an activity that we are responsible for, a duty we perform to please or appease God. There can be an element of charm, of childish sincerity in this, but true prayer eschews the sentimental. We have been summoned to a spiritual maturity in which, as St Peter tells us, we are 'alive with the life of God' (1 Pet. 4.6). Now if he, St Paul, and the New Testament as a whole deserve to be taken seriously, we are led to say that prayer is something greater than our talking to God, or imagining God, or imagining holy thoughts. Indeed, as St Paul said, this cannot be a real explanation of prayer if it is true that we do not even know how to pray. But as he goes on to say, 'the Spirit is pleading for us in our inmost being beyond words, beyond thoughts, beyond images, with sighs too deep for words' (Rom. 8.26).

Prayer then, is the life of the Spirit of Jesus within our human heart: the Spirit through whose anointing we are incorporate in the Body of Christ and by which, in turn, we are returning fully awakened to the Father. We are praying when we are awakening to the presence of this Spirit in our heart. If this is so, there can be no forms or methods of prayer. There is only prayer, the stream of love between the Spirit of the risen Jesus and His Father, in which we are incorporate. If this is so, there is no part-time or partial prayer as if the Spirit were not always alive in our heart. But there are times, our twice-daily meditation, when we make a complete turn of consciousness towards this ever-present reality. There comes a level of awakening to which St Paul was clearly directing the Thessalonians when he told them to 'pray without ceasing' (1 Thess. 5.17), when our awareness of this reality is constant throughout the most diverse activities or concerns.

Just as the Eucharist is both a commemoration and an actual present event so the mantra spans levels of consciousness and dimensions of time. It is, in a sense, our echoing response to the love-cry of the Spirit, to the whole life of Jesus returning to the Father, a response not at any level of conceptual reasoning but an absolute, an unconditional response. Insofar as we are aware of it, it is a response at the deepest level of our being where we acknowledge and experience our complete poverty and complete dependence upon the sustaining love of God. Our response achieves this absolute value, travels to this source level of our being to the extent that we say the mantra with complete simplicity and persevere in our renunciation, at the time of our meditation, of our thoughts, imaginations, of our very self-consciousness. As

the mantra becomes rooted more deeply and thoroughly integrated with our consciousness , so does our whole being participate in our response to the Spirit. Its purpose is that integration
of all our levels of being with the source of our being, the source
that calls the whole person back into itself, awakened through
the Spirit of Jesus.

Our aim is the realization of our whole being and this is why
we are impelled to transcend all qualities and faculties to find
the ground of our being wherein our essential unity, the essence
of our personhood, consists. There is no doubt of the absolute
demand of the mantra. In essence it is our acceptance of the
absoluteness of God's love flooding our heart through the Spirit
of the risen Jesus. Our death consists in the relentless simplicity
of the mantra and the absolute renunciation of thought and
language at the time of our meditation.

This is not an esoteric doctrine or method. The mantra has
been in the Christian tradition of prayer from the beginning and
the understanding that prayer is beyond the operations of the
mind is to be found in every authoritative statement. St Bonaven-
ture wrote that, 'if this passover is to be perfect, we must set aside
all discursive operations of the intellect and turn the very apex
of our soul to God to be entirely transformed in Him' (*Journey of
the Soul to God* VII). Bernard Lonergan has drawn a distinction
between what is conscious and what is known. By 'conscious' he
means the experience in itself, by 'known' our understanding
and evaluation of the experience (cf. B. Lonergan, *Insight*, Darton
Longman & Todd, 1978). Now just as the Spiritual Exercises of
St Ignatius demand a clear distinction between prayer and review
(cf. B. O'Leary, 'Repetition and Review', *The Way*, Supplement
27, pp. 48–58), so this distinction of Lonergan's indicates how
we must arrange our priorities. Of course, the Christian mystery contains both our experience and our understanding of
the experience. Jesus is the whole human being summoning us

to wholeness, but unless we accept the distinction between the conscious and the known, between prayer and review, we have not admitted our own essential creatureliness. Hence, we remain bound by the limitations of that creatureliness; we have not transcended ourselves.

Again, it is not enough to give this notional assent. It must be a truth of our being apprehended by our whole being. The mantra creates the possibility of such an integration. It prepares us as a living sacrifice to the Lord. It leads us in all simplicity to the seminal Christian experience of the prayer of the Spirit in our heart. The fruits of that experience are the fruits of the Spirit, and perhaps the first discovery we make that opens the way to all these gifts of the Spirit is that of our own personal and infinite lovableness. We cannot manufacture or anticipate the experience; we can only learn to be still, to be silent and to wait with an ever-growing sense of our own harmony. Nor can we forge the gifts of the Spirit within a fabricated joyfulness, within dogmatism rather than authority, or uniformity rather than liberty. For these are mere imitations of the true Christian qualities, and they contradict the very gospel they purport to proclaim.

The authentic Christian qualities, the fruits of the Spirit, are given with and grow out of the experience of the Spirit of Jesus, flooding our hearts with God's personal love and summoning us to the fullness of our personhood in our personal encounter with Jesus: 'By their fruits you shall know them.' The renewal and enrichment of the Church and its reinstatement as an authoritative voice in human lives depends upon its members' receiving this experience in the depths of their own hearts. Each member of the Church is called to this awakening as a present reality. Each of us will receive it in the way suited to our own unique personhood, within the plan for our fulfilment held in the mysterious love of God.

I do not wish to imply that meditation is the only way, but

rather that it is the only way I have found. In my own experience it is the way of pure simplicity that enables us to become fully, integrally aware of the Spirit Jesus has sent into our heart; and this is the recorded experience of the mainstream of the Christian tradition from Apostolic times down to our own day.

THE FATHER

Romans 8.15

If the gospel of Jesus were ever to be established as the basis of a political system, humanity would have achieved one of its perennial ideals, the self-renewing revolution. But first it would have to become a reality in our personal lives for the Kingdom of God on earth begins in the human heart: 'Be converted in heart and believe the gospel.' This is the lynchpin of all idealism, that it has first to be realized in the individual life and then, and then only, can it be presented as the means of general salvation.

This means that we have to be able ourselves to recognize the life of God in all situations and peoples, to identify it for a sceptical generation looking for signs elsewhere, and then to place it in the context of that ultimate revelation of God's life which Jesus brought to us all in His own person. To see God in the world, in other faiths, in our lonely cities and dismal suburbs, we have first to have found the image of God in ourselves. We are then free to accept the generosity of God's love wherever it overflows from the depths of His own being. We need that sensitive spirit of liberty of which St Paul wrote to the Galatians: 'If you are led by the Spirit, you are not under the law' (Gal. 5.18).

I have been suggesting in this book that meditation affirms the essential naturalness of spiritual growth. Because Jesus has already passed beyond the veil in His human form and nature, it remains for us only to realize the life He has made available to us, to activate our potential by enlightenment and enlargement of our consciousness. The light that enlightens us bathes the whole of creation but it enters us through a narrow aperture. 'The gate that leads to life is small and the road is narrow' (Matt. 7.13), said Jesus. It is narrow because it is the product of concentration, the focusing of our whole being, all our energies and faculties upon a single point.

Sartre wrote that, 'the only thing that counts is total commitment'. It is certainly the only thing that authenticates our efforts and proves our sincerity. The way to fullness of life is just this way of total commitment of our personhood to the Other, the complete and harmonious concentration of mind, body and spirit upon the centre of our being. The beliefs and values we take with us into the silence of this commitment are, as Thomas Merton often said, of limited importance because they are largely the familiar compounds of language and imagination. But we all know in our heart that the riddle of our existence is solved beyond these compounds, by focusing upon the centre of our being where we in some way know our source and meaning to lie.

We cannot, strictly speaking, achieve or acquire this integral condition of commitment and concentration. As St Paul said we do not know how to pray. There are no tricks or devices that will get quick results, no instant mysticism, or at least none that will not overload an unprepared and undisciplined psyche. But there is a way for us to prepare ourselves for the emergence, in a natural process which is itself the gift of God, of the light of the Spirit. The mantra stills the mind and summons all our faculties to the resolution of a single point; that point we know as the condition of complete simplicity which demands not less than everything.

It is only when we have focused everything, surrendered everything that we are able to receive everything. Until then, the real generosity, the superabundance of the gospel message does not strike us as credible. We are numbed by the extravagance of the claims put by the New Testament writers and we read them as metaphor or tone them down in safe theological formulae. But the essence of the message of Jesus is an unlimited generosity, a complete self-giving of the infinite God. This is proclaimed throughout the New Testament: 'He who unites himself with the Lord becomes one spirit with Him' (1 Cor. 6.17); 'Then I shall know fully, even as I have been fully understood' (Rom. 13.12); 'Here and now we are God's heirs. What we shall be like has not yet been disclosed, but we shall be like Him for we shall see Him as He is' (1 John 3.2).

If Jesus had not Himself told us that whatever He has received from the Father He gives to us, we could never have dared to believe it. Indeed, few want to believe it because, at least at the conceptual level (that is, before the beginning of personal veri-fication) it seems to suggest the swallowing up of the person in God. It is only when we are led by the Spirit, when we take our first steps in the actual experience that we begin to understand what Teilhard de Chardin meant in saying that, 'in every domain, union differentiates'. In the superabundance of love, we become the person we are called to be.

Jesus explained His own mission as the proclamation of the Father: the revelation to humanity of the person whom He en-countered in the depths of His own human heart. His union with all human beings, His calling us friends, brothers and sisters, His loving all-embracing universalization through the Spirit: all these considerations serve to confirm what He Himself assured us of, that we are called to the same knowledge and the same commun-ion with the Father, the same completion and verification of our being that He enjoyed in his human nature and communicates to us as the incarnate Word. When He sends the Spirit into our hearts, Jesus transmits to us everything that He receives from the Father (John 15.15). He withholds nothing, neither any secret nor intimacy of personal love. By His very nature He is impelled to give all of Himself, and the power, the urgency of the love-impulse radiating from the Father make it impossible for Jesus to retain any area of special privilege, of non-communication. The building up of the Body of Christ is precisely the consuming desire of Jesus to flood every part of our human consciousness with His Spirit. Nothing can prevent that desire from being satisfied except our reluctance or fear to receive, to acknowledge, to awaken to this gift of God's personal love.

The heart of the Christian mystery, of the life of Jesus Himself, is the mysterious paradox of life proceeding from death. But to avoid being overwhelmed by the unresolvable paradox and lapsing into either extreme of superstition or cynicism, we need a personal inner balance, what Scripture calls one of the gifts of the Spirit: self-control. This is precisely the fruit of meditation, the middle way, the centring process of silent prayer. But this is very different from mere passivity or quietism. The awakening of our own spirit to the Spirit of Jesus cannot be received by us passively, as if it were a pre-packaged experience imported from outside, or as if we were not persons created in the image of God but objects masquerading as persons. Our awakening is, in itself, the awareness of our participation in the life of God, of God as the source of our personhood, the very power by which we are enabled to accept His gift of our being. It is therefore a free response, an utterly personal communication, a free acceptance.

Our beginning and our end lie in the infinite generosity of God, that extravagance of love in which divinity transcends itself in each of God's self-manifestations. The human mind is not constituted to be able to make complete sense of this. We can, it is true, glimpse the nature of transcendence by our sensitivity to paradox. But we always return to the fact of God's unimaginable generosity, such generosity which, even in the human experience, is the source of liberty and joy. We are indeed most God-like when we give ourselves without measure, when, that is to say, we love; and it is without measure that God's self-giving reaches us (John 3.34). God has 'lavished' His Spirit upon us; God's love has 'flooded' our hearts.

If it keeps this vision central to its work, any theological investigation must lead to a sense of awe, of wonder, of joy, and to a humility that liberates us from all our own petty self-importance; for it should lead us to an awareness of the God who is both infinitely beyond us and yet closer to us than we are to ourselves. Any discussion about God has value to the degree that it is truly a revelation. This, I think, is what Evagrius Ponticus meant when he said that, 'if you are a theologian you truly pray, if you truly pray you are a theologian' (*Chapters on Prayer* 60).

Meditation is not a technique of prayer. It is, though, an incredibly simple means of leading us into an integral awareness of the nature of our own being and of the central, authenticating fact of our being which is the Spirit praying 'Abba, Father' in our heart. I say 'simple' not 'easy'. The way of simplicity soon becomes a pilgrimage in which we will experience the difficulty of laying down our lives. But we are not alone on the pilgrimage. We have both the community of the faithful and persevering, and the guidance of the Spirit in our heart. To the degree that we lay ourselves down, to the same degree and a hundredfold will we be restored to ourselves. The fruit of the radical simplicity of the mantra is a joy beyond description and a peace beyond understanding.

The multiplicities of thought and the mobility of words all find their resolution in the little word, the mantra. John Cassian described it as 'embracing all the feelings implanted in human nature' and as 'comprising all our thoughts' (*Conference* 10.10, 12). When it is rooted in us, the mantra leads us to that point of unity where we become simple enough to see, to receive, and to know the infinite gift of God's personal love. It leads us to that joy promised by Jesus to those who persevere on the pilgrimage to simplicity, the same joy St Paul wished to the Philippians: 'I wish you all joy in the Lord, I will say it again: all joy be yours. Let your magnanimity be manifest to all ... . The grace of our Lord Jesus Christ be with your spirit' (Phil. 4.4–5, 23).

Twelve Steps for Meditators

This section is intended to help you prepare for the silence of meditation. It is designed to help you bring your mind to a state of peacefulness, to concentration. It is meant to point you in the direction you need to be facing for your meditation, which is centrewards, to help you to move on and also to set out once more with faith and love and openness on your pilgrimage with the freshness of a new start. In meditation we are all beginners.

There are twelve separate pieces here, and my recommendation is that you read just one of them at a time, and then begin your meditation.

Remember, to meditate well you need the quietest place you can find. You need a good posture, with your spine upright and calm, and regular breathing. Then begin to say your mantra calmly, peacefully, and with complete simplicity. To meditate you need only to repeat your mantra with persevering faithfulness.

These pieces are not designed to provide you with something to think about during your meditation, but are meant as an encouragement for you to persevere and to be faithful. If you can concentrate on each one for five minutes or so you will be preparing yourself in the art of meditation, which is essentially concentration. But in your meditation you will not then be concentrating on ideas or images. You will be concentrating on the mantra and the silence to which it will lead you.

The Tradition of the Mantra I

I have often found when I have talked to people about meditation that it is the non-Christian, even the person with no religion, who first understands what meditation is about. To many ordinary churchgoers and many priests, monks and sisters, the mantra seems at first a suspiciously new-fangled technique of prayer or like some exotic trick-method, or some kind of therapy that may help you to relax, but has no claim to be called Christian. This is a desperately sad state of affairs. So many Christians have lost touch with their own tradition of prayer. We no longer benefit as we should from the wisdom and experienced counsel of the great masters of prayer. All these masters have agreed that in prayer it is not we ourselves who are taking the initiative. We are not talking to God. We are listening to God's Word within us. We are not looking for God, it is God who has found us. Walter Hilton expressed it very simply in the fourteenth century. He wrote: 'You, yourself, do nothing, you simply allow Him to work in your soul' (*The Scale of Perfection*, Bk II, ch. 24 – see Bibliography). The advice of St Teresa was in tune with this. She reminds us that all we can do in prayer is to dispose ourselves; the rest is in the power of the Spirit who leads us.

The language in which we express our spiritual experience changes. The reality of the Spirit does not change. So it is not enough to read the masters of prayer; we have to be able to apply the criterion of our own experience, limited though it may be, in order to see the same reality shining through different testimonies. For example, what Hilton and St Teresa are showing us is the same experience of prayer as that which led St Paul to write that 'we do not even know how to pray, but the Spirit prays within us' (Rom. 8.26). What this means in the language of our own day is that before we can pray we have first to become still, to concentrate. Only then can we enter into a loving awareness of the Spirit of Jesus within our heart. Now many Christians would still say at this point, 'Very well, but this is for Saints, for specialists in prayer,' as if stillness and silence were not universal elements of the human spirit. This type of obstinate false humility is based on a plain unawareness of who St Paul was writing to in Rome and Corinth and Ephesus. He was not writing to specialists, to Carmelites and Carthusians, but to husbands, wives, butchers and bakers. It shows too an unawareness of the specific teaching on prayer by later masters.

St Teresa of Avila, for example, was of the opinion that if you were serious about prayer, you would be led into what she called 'the prayer of quiet' within a relatively short time, six months or a year. Abbot Marmion saw the first year's novitiate in the monastery as being designed to lead at the end of it to what he called 'contemplative prayer'. St John of the Cross said that the principal sign of your readiness for silence in prayer was that your discursive thinking at the time of prayer was becoming evidently a distraction and counter-productive. Yet there is a kind of self-important posing humility that makes us stand aloof from the call of the redemptive love of Jesus. Very often we are reluctant to admit that we are the sick and sinful Jesus came to heal, and very often we prefer our self-protecting isolation to the risk of our face-to-face encounter with the Other in the silence of our own vulnerability.

In meditation we turn the searchlight of consciousness off

ourselves and that means off a self-centred analysis of our own unworthiness. 'If memories of past actions keep coming between you and God', says the author of *The Cloud of Unknowing*, 'you are resolutely to step over them because of your deep love for God' (*The Cloud of Unknowing*, ch. 6). In prayer we come to a deeper awareness of God in Christ. Our way is the way of silence. The way to silence is the way of the mantra.

The Tradition of the Mantra II

Jesus summons us to fullness of life, not to a self-centred reluctance to realize the true beauty and wonder of our being. The mantra is an ancient tradition, the purpose of which is to accept the invitation Jesus makes.

We find it in the ancient Jewish custom of 'blessing the Lord at all times'. We find the mantra in the early Christian Church. We may find it, for example, in the Our Father which was a series of short rhythmic phrases in the original Aramaic. We find it too in the Orthodox tradition of the Jesus Prayer, the prayer that Jesus Himself commended: 'Lord, be merciful to me, a sinner' (Luke 18.13). The prayer of Jesus Himself as recorded in the Gospel leads to the same conclusions. 'Lord, teach us to pray,' the disciples asked Him. His teaching was simplicity itself: 'When you pray do not be like the hypocrites . . . but go into a room by yourself, shut the door and pray to your Father who is there in the secret place . . . Do not go babbling on like the heathen who imagine that the more they say, the more likely they are to be heard. Your Father knows what your needs are before you ask him' (Matt. 6.5–8). In the Garden of Gethsemani Jesus is described as praying over and over again 'in the same words' (Mark 14.39, Matt. 26.44) and whenever He addresses the Father for the sake of the crowd, the word, 'Abba', is always on His lips, the same word which St Paul describes the Spirit of Jesus eternally crying in our hearts.

Time and again the practical advice of masters of prayer is summed up in the simple injunction: 'Say your mantra'; 'Use this little word'. *The Cloud of Unknowing* advises, 'and pray not in many words but in a little word of one syllable. Fix this word fast to your heart so that it is always there come what may. With this word you will suppress all thoughts' (*The Cloud of Unknowing*, ch. 7, 39). Abbot Chapman, in his famous letter of Michaelmas 1920 from Downside, describes the simple, faithful use of a mantra which he had rediscovered more from his own courageous perseverance in prayer than from teachers. He had rediscovered a simple enduring tradition of prayer that entered the West through monasticism, and first entered Western monasticism through John Cassian in the late fourth century. Cassian himself received it from the holy men of the desert who placed its origin back beyond living memory to Apostolic times.

The venerable tradition of the mantra in Christian prayer is above all attributable to its utter simplicity. It answers all the requirements of the masters' advice on how to pray because it leads us to a harmonious, attentive stillness of mind, body and spirit. It requires no special talent or gift apart from serious intent and the courage to persevere. 'No one', Cassian said, 'is kept away from purity of heart by not being able to read nor is rustic simplicity any obstacle to it for it lies close at hand for all if only they will by constant repetition of this phrase keep the mind and the heart attentive to God' (*Conference* 10.14). Our mantra is the ancient Aramaic prayer, 'Maranatha, Maranatha'. 'Come Lord. Come Lord Jesus'.

Saying the Mantra I

Learning to meditate is learning to say the mantra, and because it is as simple as this, we should be quite clear in our understanding of the process of saying the mantra.

We must grow in our fidelity to the mantra and in the same proportion the mantra will grow more and more deeply rooted in us. As you know, the mantra I recommend you to say is the word 'Maranatha', the ancient Aramaic prayer which means 'Come Lord. Come Lord Jesus'. I suggest that you articulate it in your mind silently, with equal stress on each of the four syllables. Ma-ra-na-tha. We usually begin by saying the mantra, that is, it seems as though we are speaking it with our mind silently, somewhere in our head, but as we make progress the mantra becomes more familiar, less of a stranger, less of an intruder in our consciousness. We find less effort is required to persevere in saying it throughout the time of our meditation. Then it seems that we are not so much speaking it in our minds as sounding it in our heart, and this is the stage that we describe as the mantra becoming rooted in our hearts.

No metaphor is really very satisfactory in this matter but it is sometimes helpful and reassuring to know that one's own experience in meditation is also the general experience of the faithful. So, at this stage of sounding the mantra in our hearts, we might describe it as similar to pushing lightly a pendulum that needs only a slight stimulus to set it swinging in a calm, steady rhythm. It is at this moment that our meditation is really beginning. We are really beginning to concentrate away from ourselves because from now on, instead of either saying or sounding the mantra, we begin to listen to it, wrapped in ever-deepening attention. When he described this stage of meditation, my teacher used to say that from this moment on it is as though the mantra is sounding in the valley below us while we are toiling up the side of a mountain.

Meditation is in essence the art of concentration precisely because, the higher we toil up the mountain side, the fainter becomes the mantra sounding in the valley below us, and so the more attentively and seriously we have to listen to it. There then comes the day when we enter that 'cloud of unknowing' in which there is silence, absolute silence, and we can no longer hear the mantra.

But we must always remember that we cannot attempt to force the pace of meditation in any way or to speed up the natural process in which the mantra roots itself in our consciousness by means of our simple fidelity in saying it. We must not be self-consciously asking ourselves, 'How far have I got? Am I saying the mantra or sounding it or listening to it?' If we try to force the pace or to keep a constant self-conscious eye on our progress we are, if there is such a word, non-meditating because we are con-centrating on ourselves, putting ourselves first, thinking about ourselves. Meditation requires complete simplicity. We are led to that complete simplicity, but we begin and continue by saying the mantra.

Saying the Mantra II

I need to stress here the importance of continuing to say the man-tra because, when we start to meditate we can often come quite quickly into realms of peacefulness and experience a sense of pleasant well-being, even euphoria; saying the mantra can then be made to appear a distraction. We do not want to lose this pleas-ant plateau and so we try to stay where we are, to strike camp and make no further progress up the mountain side. We stop saying the mantra. Many people are led into long, unnecessarily long, and uncreative periods when they make no progress for this very reason. They barter the potential of an expanding consciousness and a deepening awareness of the Spirit for a kind of floating piety, a kind of religious anaesthesia.

The great fourth-century master of prayer, our master, John Cassian, had already noted this danger in alluding to what he called, the '*pax perniciosa*', the pernicious peace. His graphic phrase points out something that needs to be remembered if we ever think that we can just say, 'So far and no further, this will do'. *Perniciosa* means what it says, namely, destructive or fatal. I am myself convinced that many people do not make the progress they should in prayer, and do not become as free as they are called to be in prayer, simply because they opt for this destructive lethargy, they give up too soon in their toilsome pilgrimage up the mountain side; they abandon the constant saying of the mantra.

When we begin to meditate we must say the mantra for the whole twenty or thirty minutes of our meditation, regardless of whatever mood we are in or whatever reaction we seem to be having. As we progress in fidelity in saying it, we must then sound it for the whole time of our meditation, whatever the distractions or feelings that may arise. Then, as the mantra becomes rooted in our heart, we must listen to it with our whole attention without ceasing.

I repeat this to re-emphasize what is the essential and perhaps the only advice worth giving about meditation, which is simply: *to say your mantra*. This is not an easy doctrine to accept, nor is it easy to follow. We all hope when we first begin to meditate for some instant mystical experience, and we tend to over-estimate the first unusual experiences that the process of meditation brings to us. But this is not important. The important thing is to persevere with the mantra, to stabilize ourselves by our discipline which makes us ready for the higher slopes of the mountain.

We need not be over-concerned with our motives to begin with. It is not we, but the Lord who takes the initiative. As John Cassian puts it: 'He, Himself, has struck the small spark of good will out of the hard flints of our hearts.' So, now, begin your meditation in simplicity of heart and be faithful to your humble task of saying the mantra without ceasing.

Leaving Self Behind

These are the words of Jesus taken from St Mark's Gospel: 'Anyone who wishes to be a follower of mine must leave self behind; he must take up his cross and come with me' (Mark 8.34). Now we meditate to do just that: to obey that absolutely fundamental call Jesus makes, which is the basis of all our Christian faith, to leave self behind in order that we can indeed journey with Christ in His return to the Father.

Saying the mantra is a discipline which helps us to transcend all the limitations of our narrow and isolated self-obsession. The mantra leads us into an experience of the liberty that reigns at the centre of our being. 'Where the Spirit is there is liberty' (2 Cor. 3.17), said St Paul. It introduces us to this liberty by helping us to pass over into the Other, by helping us to take our minds off ourselves. This is what Jesus means by leaving self behind.

In our own day we have perhaps lost our understanding of what it really means to renounce self. Self-renunciation is not an experience with which our contemporaries are familiar or which they even understand very clearly, mainly because the tendency of our society is to emphasize the importance of self-promotion, self-preservation, self-projection. The materialism of our consumer society puts 'What I want' at the centre of our life, and it renders 'the other' merely an object which we see in terms of our own pleasure or advantage. But the other is only really Other if approached with reverence for itself and in itself. We must learn to pay complete attention to it and not to its effect upon us. If we begin to objectify the other then its reality, its uniqueness, and essential value escape us and it becomes not the other, but a projection of ourselves.

Many people today and in the past have confused self-renunciation with self-rejection. But our meditation is no running away from, no attempt to evade the responsibility of our own being or the responsibilities of our life and relationships. Meditation is rather an affirmation of ourselves, not however of the self that is involved in this particular responsibility alone, nor the self that wants this or wants that. These aspects of our self are illusory; they become little egos when we isolate them from the central point of our being where our irreducible selfhood exists in complete harmony with the Other, the Other being the source of our being and the sustainer of our selfhood. It is this whole self, the real self which we affirm in the silence of meditation.

We cannot affirm it however by trying to lay violent hands on it or by trying to possess or control it. If we do so, we are in the absurd position of our ego trying to command the self, or unreality dictating to reality, or of the tail wagging the dog. This is what Niebuhr meant when he said: 'The self does not realize itself fully when self-realization is the conscious aim.' In meditating we affirm ourselves by becoming still, by becoming silent, we allow the reality of our real self to become more and more apparent; we allow its light to diffuse throughout our being in the course of the natural process of spiritual growth. We do not try to do anything. We simply let ourselves be. When we are renouncing self, we are in that condition of liberty and receptivity that allows us to be in relationship with the Other, which is the condition that makes it possible for us to decide positively for the Other, to say, though not in words, 'I love you.'

But we can only turn to the Other, we can only make this

movement of self, if we leave self behind, that is, if we take our consciousness away from its involvement with me and direct it on the thou. Self-obsession is the means of restricting and limiting the self. Self-renunciation, on the other hand, is the means of liberating the self for its real purpose which is loving the Other. Meditation is a simple and natural process. It is the process that reveals our real being as a state of open-hearted receptivity to the Spirit of Jesus who dwells in our hearts. This revelation dawns when we renounce, step aside from, the eternal manifestations of our consciousness such as thoughts, words and images and when instead we move into the level of consciousness itself. We then become silent because we have entered silence and we are wholly turned towards the Other. In this fully conscious, fully free silence, we naturally open ourselves to the Word that proceeds from the silence, God's own Word, in whom we are called into being, and in which we ourselves are spoken by the Creator.

This is the living Word within us. Our faith tells us that we are wholly incorporate in this Word, but we need to know it fully, in the height, length, depth and breadth of our spirit, to know it though it is beyond knowledge. The silence brings us to this knowledge that is so simple that no thought or image could ever contain or represent it. By renouncing self we enter the silence and focus upon the Other. The truth to be revealed is the harmony of our Self with the Other. In the words of the Sufi poet: 'I saw my Lord with my heart's eye and said: "Who art Thou Lord?" "Thyself," He replied.'

John Cassian

We would not still be reading the Gospels or St Paul today, were it not true that the human experience of the Spirit is essentially the same at all times and in all traditions, because it is, in essence, the same encounter with the redemptive love of God in Jesus Christ, who is the same yesterday, today and forever. The importance of this truth for us today is that although no one can make another's pilgrimage for him, we can nevertheless benefit from the experience and the wisdom of those who have made the pilgrimage before us. In His own day and for His contemporaries, Jesus was seen as just such a teacher who had reached enlightenment through His fidelity and perseverance.

Throughout Christian history, men and women of prayer have fulfilled a special mission in bringing their contemporaries, and even succeeding generations, to the same enlightenment, the same rebirth in Spirit that Jesus preached. One of these teachers, John Cassian, of the fourth century, has a claim to be one of the most influential teachers of the spiritual life in the West. His special importance as the teacher and inspirer of St Benedict and so of the whole of Western monasticism, derives from the part he played in bringing the spiritual tradition of the East into the living experience of the West.

Cassian's own pilgrimage began with his own search for a teacher, for a master of prayer, a master he could not find in his own monastery in Bethlehem. Just as thousands of young people today make their pilgrimage to the East in search of wisdom and personal authority, so Cassian and his friend Germanus journeyed to the deserts of Egypt where the holiest and most famous spiritual teachers of their time were to be found. In his *Institutes* and *Conferences* Cassian himself hardly comes across as a distinct personality, no more than St Benedict does in his Rule which is so heavily indebted to John Cassian. But we do feel that we are encountering a spirit in Cassian: one which, like St Benedict's, has achieved the object of its own teaching, the transcendence of self.

Cassian's special qualities, that give him such authority and directness, are his capacity to listen and his gift of communicating what he has heard and made his own. It was in listening with total attention to the teaching of the holy Abbot Isaac that Cassian was first fired with an enthusiasm for prayer and the firm resolve to persevere. Abbot Isaac spoke eloquently and sincerely but, as Cassian concludes in his first *Conference*: 'With these words of the Holy Isaac we were dazzled rather than satisfied, since we felt that though the excellence of prayer had been shown to us still we had not yet understood its nature and the power by which continuance in it might be gained and kept' (*Conference* 9.36).

His experience was clearly similar to that of many today who have heard inspiring accounts of prayer but are left uninstructed as to the practical means of really becoming aware of the Spirit praying in their hearts. Cassian and Germanus humbly returned to Abbot Isaac after a few days with the simple question: 'How do we pray? Teach us, show us.' His answer to their question, which can be found in Cassian's tenth *Conference*, had a decisive influence on the Western understanding of prayer down to our own day. It shows, firstly, that prayer is both the acknowledgement and experience of our own poverty, our own utter dependence on God who is the source of our being. But it is also the experience of our redemption, our enrichment by the love of God in Jesus. These related aspects of prayer, of poverty and redemption leads Cassian to call the condition we enjoy in prayer a 'grand poverty'. 'The mind should unceasingly cling to the mantra', Cassian writes, 'until strengthened by continual use of it, it casts off and rejects the rich and ample matter of all kinds of thought and restricts itself to the poverty of the single verse . . . Those who realize this poverty arrive with ready ease at the first of the beatitudes: 'Blessed are they who are poor in spirit for theirs is the Kingdom of Heaven' (ibid. 10.11).

The spiritual life for Cassian, the serious perseverance in the poverty of the single verse, is a passover. By persevering we pass from sorrow to joy, from loneliness to communion. And, unlike many of the Egyptian ascetics who saw mortification as an end in itself, Cassian clearly teaches that it is merely a means to an end and that end is the unbroken awareness of the life of the Spirit continually renewing us, giving new life to our mortal bodies. Similarly, he sees the religious community as a means of leading each individual to an awareness of his communion with all in Jesus. Just as the mantra is the sacrament of our poverty in prayer, so in the community absolute honesty and frankness in our relationships with one another and above all with our teacher are the signs and means of making the passover from fear to love.

One of the recurrent themes of Cassian is the absolute importance of personal verification. We must know for ourselves in the depth of our own being. We must perform rather than teach, be rather than do. Above all, we must be fully awake to the wonder and beauty of our being, to the mystery of the personal life of Jesus in our heart. Relentlessly, we must avoid the pitfall of half consciousness, the drowsy state of what he calls pernicious peace, *pax perniciosa*, a lethal sleep, the *sopor letalis*. His importance as a teacher in our own day is his simplicity and directness, for his are noble sentiments, inspiring ideals. But how do we fulfil the command of Jesus, 'to stay awake and pray' (Matt. 26.41)? Cassian brought the answer to the West from the ancient tradition of Christian prayer. By knowing ourselves to be poor and by deepening in prayer our experience of poverty in complete self-renunciation. The simple practical means he teaches is the unceasing use of the mantra. He wrote that the Christian's principal aim is the realization of the Kingdom of God, the power of the Spirit of Jesus in our heart. But we cannot achieve this by our own efforts or think our way into it and so we have a simpler more immediate goal which he calls 'purity of heart' (*Conference* 1.4). This is all we should concern ourselves with, he teaches. The rest will be given to us. And the way to purity of heart, to full and clear awareness, is the way of poverty, the 'grand poverty' of the mantra.

Set Your Mind on the Kingdom

If most of us were asked why we thought we were not fulfilled, why we were not simply happy, we would probably not answer using terms such as essential harmony, awareness, consciousness or spirit. We would be much more likely to point to particular features of our life such as work, relationships, or health, and to attribute our unhappiness or anxiety to one or all of these. Many people, indeed, would not even see all these different aspects of their life as having any common point of contact. To so many of us the activities of our day are like parallel lines and many actively resent one area's impinging on another. The result of this is that modern life so often lacks a centre, a point of convergence, a source of unity. Consequently, men and women lose the sense of their own creative centre and as a result they have no contact with their real selves.

The understanding of prayer that makes it merely a matter of telling God what we want or need and reminding God of our sins of omission only compounds our alienation from reality. For this was the liberating message Jesus came to bring: 'I bid you put away anxious thought about food or drink to keep you alive and clothes to cover your body. Surely life is more than food, the body more than clothes' (Matt. 6.25). What Jesus is advocating here is not an irresponsible or fanatical indifference to the external aspects of our life, but rather He is urging us to develop a spirit of trust; of absolute trust, in the Fatherhood and Motherhood of the God who not only created us, but sustains us in being from moment to moment. 'Do not be anxious about tomorrow; tomorrow will look after itself,' He taught (Matt. 6.34). Realize yourself, that is, in the present moment because your happiness and fulfilment are here and now.

To trust another is to renounce self and place your centre of gravity in the other. This is liberty and this is love. 'All these things', said Jesus of the material concerns of life, 'are for the heathen to run after, not for you, because your heavenly Father knows that you have need of all of them.' The trust which He calls on His followers to have in the loving inclusiveness of God is not the immature, childish presumption of getting what you want simply because you want it. To trust in God means to have turned ourselves fully towards another and if we have done that we have transcended both ourselves and our wanting. In this experience of transcendence itself we receive more than we could ever have asked for or ever have dared even to want: 'Set your mind on God's Kingdom before everything else, and all the rest will come to you as well' (Matt. 6.33).

The proper ordering of our external activities can only be achieved once we have re-established conscious contact with the centre of all these activities and concerns. This centre is the aim of our meditation. It is the centre of our being. In St Teresa's words, 'God is the centre of the soul.' When our access to this centre is opened up, the Kingdom of God is established in our hearts. That kingdom is nothing less than the present power and all-pervasive life of God permeating all creation. In the words of John Cassian: 'God who is the author of eternity would have men ask for nothing that is uncertain, petty or temporal' (*Conference* 9.24). This is not because God does not want us to enjoy the good things of life, but because we can fully enjoy them only when we have experienced the divine self-giving from whom all good things come, who is goodness itself. The proof of His generosity is also what St Paul calls, 'The ground of our hope'. It is: 'The love of God flooding our inmost hearts through the Holy Spirit He has given us' (Rom. 5.5).

This is not an experience reserved for the selected few. It is a gift available to all men and women. To receive it we must return to the centre of our being where it enters us, to the source of our being where we find the infusion of God's love through the Spirit of Jesus.

Realizing Our Personal Harmony I

One of the most distinctive features of our time is the almost universal feeling among people that they must somehow get back to a basic level of personal confidence, to the ground or bed-rock of their life. An almost universal fear is the fear of slipping into non-being, losing touch with ourselves, living at a certain distance from ourselves. James Joyce said of one of his charac-ters that 'he lived at a certain distance from his body'. It was a marvellously simple but accurate diagnosis of what we have come to know as alienation.

The reasons for our sense of alienation from ourselves, from others, and from nature are no doubt legion, but there are per-haps two particular causes. The first is our evasion of personal responsibility. We are out of touch with ourselves because we allow someone or something else to take our personal decisions for us. How often do we say of someone when they act unconven-tionally, 'He has gone off the rails,' with the underlying assump-tion that society lays down the course that every life must follow. A second reason is the way we are trained to compartmental-ize our lives too rigidly into, for example, school, work, home, family, entertainment, church and so on. As a result we lose a sense of our own personal wholeness. The whole person is involved in any activity or responsibility we undertake, just as the personal presence of God is total everywhere and cannot be made into a partial or a limited presence.

Modern people are in a state of deep confusion because the complexity and fractionalization of their lives seem to have destroyed their personhood. The question we ask, which is asked by all modern men and women and not just by religious people, is: 'How can we get back into touch with ourselves? How do we recover a sense of confidence in ourselves, the confidence of knowing that we really do exist in our own right?' It is a question we must ask and answer, because without this basic confidence in our own existence we have not the courage to go out from ourselves to meet the other, and without the other we do not become fully ourselves.

There is also a kind of universal instinct that warns us that the answer to this question is not found in the way of cerebral self-analysis. To discover our essential harmony and wholeness, which is what finding oneself means, we cannot concentrate on just one limited part of our being. The particular rediscovery that humanity is making, though it is also a new discovery, is that reality can be known only as a whole, not in parts, and that this total apprehension can be realized only in silence. We see this truth being discovered in many areas of life and thought today. Abstract art, for example, defies or renounces any meaningful linguistic equivalent. We cannot talk about different shades of maroon on canvas. Wittgenstein, perhaps more than any other writer, has brought us to the brink of saying that language cannot be trusted to represent the truth. Speech is a kind of infinite regression for words only really refer to other words. This is a liberating discovery for each of us, provided that we can have the courage to follow it through and become truly silent. If we can do so one of our first rewards will be the awareness of our own essential harmony, the harmony we find through whole-hearted attention in prayer, and that attentiveness is something more profound, more real, than anything that thought, language or imagination can achieve. The whole person, rejoicing in life and its given-ness can find joy in his or her wholeness: 'I thank Thee Lord for the wonder of my being' (Ps. 138.13), sings the psalmist.

Our task in meditation is to allow our unity to be restored and for our scattered parts to move back into their proper harmonious alignment to the centre of our being. To do this we must not scatter ourselves further. We have to concentrate, to move towards our centre. When our consciousness truly awakens to that centre, in silence, then a power is released which is the power of life, the power of the Spirit. In that power we are reformed, reunited, re-created. 'When a person is united to the Spirit there is a new world' (2 Cor. 5.17), said St Paul. The mantra leads us straight to this centre.

Realizing Our Personal Harmony II

In the last piece I wrote about modern people becoming more and more aware of the insufficiency of language as a means of leading them to self-discovery. There is nothing ant-intellectual about this. It does not suggest that language is not an essential means of communication between people. Indeed this book would be something of an anachronism if it did suggest that. Language may not be able to lead us into the ultimate communion, but it is the atmosphere in which we first draw the breath of consciousness. It expands our consciousness and leads us to silence, but only in and through silence do we become fully conscious.

As an example of this somewhat abstract point, let me return to the idea of our personal harmony. As an idea we have to talk about it in language. Language uses words. Words have meaning to the extent that they do not mean something else and so to talk about personal harmony we must analyse, distinguish, separate. By personal harmony I mean the integration, the perfect co-

operation of mind and heart, body and spirit. But when I talk
about them like this, as separate entities, am I not suggesting that
they actually work independently of each other? Of course you
know that I know that they do not work for themselves but they
work for the whole. If I hear some joyful news I feel that joy in my
body, I know it in my mind and it expands my spirit. All these
things happen, they are altogether my response, my involvement
in what is happening to me. It is not that my body is telling my
mind something or that my mind is communicating something
to me through body language. I am a whole person and I respond
wholly (cf. 1 Cor. 12.12–36).

We know that we are this whole person, this harmony and
yet we do not know it because this knowledge has not yet become fully conscious. Perhaps we could say that the conscious
harmony that lives in perfect joy and liberty at the centre of our
being has not yet expanded and spread itself throughout our
being. To allow it to do so we must simply remove the obstacle
of narrowly self-conscious thought, self-important language. In
other words we must become silent. If we really did know ourselves as body-mind-spirit, as the harmony of these three, then
we would be on the way to making that knowledge fully conscious throughout our whole being. But as modern people, at any
rate, we have lost the knowledge of our spirit and confused it with
our mental awareness. As a result we have lost that sense of our
own balance and proportion as a creature which should lead us
into the creative silence of prayer. It is only when we have begun
to recover our awareness of spirit that we begin to understand
the intelligent mystery of our being. We are not just an extreme
of body and an extreme of mind co-existing. We have a principle
of unity within our being, in the centre of our being and it is this,
our spirit, which is the image of God within us.

The fourteenth-century author of *The Cloud of Unknowing*
writes: 'I tell you the truth when I say that this work [of medita-

tion] demands great serenity, an integrated and pure disposition in soul and body . . . God forbid that I should separate what God has coupled: the body and the spirit' (*The Cloud of Unknowing*, ch. 41, 48). The way to become fully conscious of this essential harmony of our being is to be silent. And to meditate is to be silent. The harmony of our essence, our centre, then, as it were blossoms and diffuses itself throughout every part and molecule of our being. *The Cloud* puts it very charmingly: 'When grace draws people to contemplation it seems to transfigure them even physically so that though they may be ill-favoured by nature they now appear changed and lovely to behold' (*The Cloud of Unknowing*, ch. 54).

The diffusion of our essential harmony throughout our being is another way of saying that the prayer of the Spirit of Jesus wells up in our hearts, floods our hearts and overflows throughout us. This is the amazing gift we have been given by Jesus sending us His Spirit. But He does not force it on us. It is for us to recognize it and accept it, and this we do, not by being clever or self-analytical, but by being silent, by being simple. The gift is already given. We have merely to open our hearts to its infinite generosity. The mantra opens our hearts in pure simplicity. 'Do you not know', wrote St Paul to the Corinthians, 'that your body is a shrine of the indwelling Holy Spirit, and the Spirit is God's gift to you?' (1 Cor. 6.19) Meditation is simply our way to knowing it.

A Present Reality

Someone once argued that there would be no morality and no conscience if we did not have a sense of the future. If we could see only the present and lived wholly in the present moment we would achieve goodness here and now because we would be unable to postpone the moment of conversion to some indefinite future time.

Perhaps part of the explanation of the phenomenal religious impact which Judaism had on the world is that in the Hebrew language there was no future tense. This sense of the eternal presentness of God pervades both the Old and New Testaments. To Moses, God gave the divine name as: 'I AM. Tell them that I AM sends you' (Exod. 3.14). Jesus not only preached the Kingdom of Heaven as already arrived, but declared: 'before the prophets were, I am' (John 8.58). This sense of the presentness of the kingdom suffuses the testimony that St Paul proclaimed: 'Now is the day of salvation; now is the acceptable time' (2 Cor. 6.2). Now read these words from the opening paragraph of Chapter 5 of Romans and pay special attention to the tenses he uses:

> Now that we have been justified through faith, let us continue at peace with God through our Lord Jesus Christ, through whom we have been allowed to enter the sphere of God's grace, where we now stand. Let us exult in the hope of the divine splendour that is to be ours. (Rom. 5.1–2)

You will see that the main effect of this passage is to draw our attention to what condition we are in now, to draw our minds into a steady concentration on the present moment.

The extraordinary dynamism of these words and the whole of St Paul's writing is that the marvel, the splendour, the unimaginable reality of the condition we are in here and now is so overwhelming that we can hardly keep our concentration steady. We have been allowed to enter the sphere of God's grace where we now stand. Jesus has blazed the trail for us and through His own experience has incorporated us in His present state which is His glorious communion with the Father in His risen life, a life that now pervades the whole of creation. We stand in the sphere of God's grace because we are where He is and He is where we are. We are in Him and His Spirit is in us.

And yet, that passage I quoted ended with the words: 'Let us exult in the hope of the divine splendour that is to be ours.' Why do we now seem to have returned to a postponement of our entering the sphere of God's grace? Is Paul's rhetoric tripping him up and leading him to contradict himself? No, what he is saying is what Jesus was saying: 'The Kingdom of Heaven is upon you, is within you.' But you must realize this. You must let your consciousness expand and your awareness develop. We are already in the sphere of God's grace because the Spirit has been sent into our hearts. But because we have been created in the image of God we are called to self-awareness. We ourselves must become aware of what Jesus has achieved for us. We must realize the persons we already are. This is the purpose of our meditation to lead us to a full awareness of who we are, where we are, to stop hovering in the realms of eternal postponement. We must touch down in the concrete reality of the present moment where our divine splendour is revealed. We must become still. We have to learn how to pay attention steadily and continuously to the reality of our being in the here and now. Père de Caussade called this 'the sacrament of the present moment', and this is what the mantra leads us into, a full awareness of the divine splendour of the eternal present. The mantra is our sacrament of the present moment.

Christian Community I

If we Christians fail today to proclaim the gospel of Jesus with sufficient conviction and enthusiasm, it is due above all to our forgetting that the very essence of our meaning is to exist for others. The Church does not exist to perpetuate itself, to guard itself against injury, to increase its own security. It exists to lead others into an awareness of the redemptive love of God in Jesus and, insofar as it does really exist for the other, the Church is invulnerable, triumphant. 'You are the light for all the world,' Jesus told His disciples. 'When a lamp is lit it is not put under the meal-tub, but on the lamp-stand, where it gives light to everyone in the house. And you, like the lamp, must shed light among your fellows, so that, when they see the good you do, they may give praise to your Father in heaven' (Matt. 5.14).

If the world does not believe what we say about Jesus, what we say about the reality of the human spirit, is it not mainly because they do not believe that we really believe it and know it? It is not enough to turn our minds to changing the image of the Church in the world, to be constantly thinking what effect will this have, what impression will that make. We have to begin not by chang-ing the image of the Church, but by rediscovering ourselves as the image of God.

There is only one way to do this and it is the essential means of shedding the light with which the Church is entrusted upon every one in the house. This is the way of prayer. The means, in this matter as in all, have to be conformable to the end. Our Christian communities do not exist for themselves, but for others and ultimately for the Other. In our prayer we have to discover ourselves existing for the Other because it is in prayer that we experience ourselves being created and sustained by Him.

In our prayer then, we let God be; we rejoice in God's being who God is; we do not try to manipulate, to harangue or to flatter God; we do not dispel God with our clever words and formulae but we worship, that is, we acknowledge God's value and worth and in so doing we discover that we, created in the image of God, share in that same value and worth as children of God.

Everyone has experienced at some time in their life, when they were with the person they loved, or perhaps at a time of deep sorrow or pain that there is a peculiar power in silence. Silence comes naturally at times of great significance in our life because we feel we are coming into a direct contact with some truth of such meaning that words would distract us, and prevent us from fully entering into that meaning. The power that silence has is to allow this truth to emerge, to rise to the surface, to become visible. It happens naturally in its own time and fashion. We know that we are not responsible for making it appear, but we know it has a personal meaning for us. We know it is greater than we are and we find a perhaps unexpected humility within ourselves that leads us to a real attentive silence. We let the truth be.

But there is also something in all of us that incites us to control others, to defuse the power we dimly apprehend in a moment of truth, to protect ourselves from its transforming power by neutralizing its otherness and imposing our own identity upon it. The crime of idolatry is precisely creating our own god in our own image and likeness. Rather than encounter God who is awesomely different from ourselves, we construct a toy model of God in our own psychic and emotional image. In doing this we do no harm to God, of course, as unreality has no power over God, but we do debase and scatter ourselves, surrendering the potential and divine glory of our humanity for the false glitter of the golden calf. The truth is so much more exciting, so much more wonderful. God is not a reflection of our consciousness but we are reflections of God, the divine image, by our incorporation with Jesus, Son of God and one of us. Our way to the experience of this truth is in the silence of our meditation.

Christian Community II

Just as we can cut God down to our own size, impose our identity on God, so we can do this with other people. Indeed, if we do it to God we inevitably do it to other people, and if we do it to them, we inevitably do it to God. This is the obverse of saying what St John said: 'If a person says "I love God" while hating his brother or sister, he is a liar. If he does not love the brother or sister whom he has seen, it cannot be that he loves God whom he has not seen. And indeed this command comes to us from Christ Himself: that whoever loves God must also love his brother and sister' (1 John 4.19–21). Let us be quite clear what St John is saying, namely that we cannot love God *or* our neighbour. We love both or neither. And what love means is rejoicing in the otherness of the other because the depth of this awareness is the depth of our communion with the other. In this communion the discovery of our own true self and that of the other is the same discovery. So, in the people we live with we find not objects to be cast in our own superficial likeness but, much more, we find in them our true selves, for our true selves only appear, only become realized, when we are wholly turned towards another.

In meditation we develop our capacity to turn our whole being towards the Other. We learn to let our neighbour be just as we learn to let God be. We learn not to manipulate our neighbour but rather to reverence them, to reverence their importance, the wonder of their being; in other words, we learn to love our neighbour. Because of this, prayer is the great school of community. In and through a common seriousness and perseverance in prayer we realize the true glory of Christian community as a brotherhood and sisterhood of the anointed, living together in profound and loving mutual respect. Christian community is in essence the experience of being held in reverence by others and we in our turn reverencing them. This reverence for each other reveals the members of the community as being sensitively attuned one to the other on the wavelength of the Spirit, the same Spirit that has called each of us to fullness of love. In others I recognize the same Spirit that lives in my heart, the Spirit that constitutes my real self. In this recognition of the other person, a recognition that remakes my mind and expands my consciousness, the other person comes into being as they really are, in their real self, not as a manipulated extension of myself. People move and act out of their own integral reality and no longer as some image created by my imagination. Even if our ideas or principles clash, we are held in unison, in dynamic equilibrium, by our mutual recognition of each other's infinite lovableness, importance and essential unique reality.

Thus the mutually supporting and suffering dynamic of Christ's mystical body has just this creative aim: the realization of each other's essential being. True community happens in the process of drawing each other into the light of true being. In this process we share a deepening experience of the joy of life, the joy of Being, as we discover more and more of its fullness in a loving faith shared with others. The essence of community then is a recognition of and deep reverence for the other. Our meditation partakes of this essence because it leads us to turn wholly towards the Other, who is the Spirit in our heart. The full revelation of otherness, and our communion with all is achieved in reverential silence. So complete is our attention to the other that we say nothing ourselves but wait for the other to speak. The mantra guides us into a deeper consciousness of the silence that reigns within us, and then supports us while we wait.

Suggested Reading

This is a deliberately short list of suggested reading. Its aim is simply to inspire you to begin the pilgrimage of meditation and persevere.

Ideally, this is done within the context of a teacher and a community. But it is important, too, to realize that the pilgrimage is followed within a universal community and one that has passed on its accumulated wisdom and insight to successive generations. The aim of these masters of prayer, whose works are recommended here, was not to provide a vicarious experience but to lead us as directly as possible into a fully personal response to the call addressed to each of us.

The most succinct, practical and balanced guide to meditation in the English mystical tradition is the anonymous fourteenth-century treatise *The Cloud of Unknowing*. The original English is brisk and vivid and has an untranslatable flavour. The best modern translation is by William Johnston in an edition that includes the same author's other work, *The Book of Privy Counselling*. It has an excellent introduction.

The best general introduction to the religious and historical context of *The Cloud of Unknowing* is David Knowles' *The Early Mystical Tradition*.

Underlying this tradition and the whole of the Western Christian tradition of prayer are the fifth-century *Conferences* of John Cassian. They retain a real vitality and contemporary relevance to the needs of our own day. The essence of Cassian's teaching on prayer is contained in the two brilliant 'Conferences of Abbot Isaac', *Conferences* 9 and 10.

One of the most inspired books of our time is *Saccidananda* by Abhishiktananda, a Benedictine monk who lived the Christian experience of prayer in India until his death in 1973. The book proclaims with unmistakable personal authority both the fully personal and fully universal nature of the Christian experience.

Bibliography

Useful editions of some of the books cited are:

1. Abhishiktananda, *Saccidananda* (a Christian approach to Advaitic Experience), I. S. P. C. K., Delhi 1974.
2. *Rule of St Benedict*. Latin text critical edition Cuthbert Butler, Herder, Freiburg 1912. There are many modern translations.
3. New English Bible, Oxford University Press with Cambridge University Press 1970.
4. John Cassian, *Institutes and Conferences*, translated by E. Gibson in 'A Select Library of Nicene and Post-Nicene Fathers of The Christian Church', Second Series, Volume XI. Wm B. Eerdmans Publishing Co., Michigan 1973.
5. *The Cloud of Unknowing*, ed. E. Underhill. Stuart and Watkins, London 1970 (original). Tr. William Johnston, Image Books, New York 1973.
6. Walter Hilton, *The Scale of Perfection*. Translated by Leo Sherley-Price, Penguin, 1957. A good modern selection is by Illtyd Trethowan O.S.B, Geoffrey Chapman, London 1975.

Works by and about John Main

Books

Awakening, London, Arthur James Ltd, 1997

Christian Meditation: The Gethsemani Talks, The World Community for Christian Meditation, 1977; Medio Media, 1999

Community of Love, London, Darton, Longman & Todd, 1990; New York, Continuum, 1999

Door to Silence, London, Canterbury Press, 2006

John Main: A Biography in Text and Photos, ed. Paul Harris, Medio Media, 2001

John Main: Essential Writings, ed. Laurence Freeman OSB, Maryknoll, NY, Orbis Books, 2002

Moment of Christ: The Path of Meditation, London, Darton, Longman & Todd, 1984; New York, Crossroad, 1984

Monastery without Walls, London, Canterbury Press, 2006

The Joy of Being: Daily Readings, London, Darton, Longman & Todd, 1987; USA, Templegate

The Heart of Creation: The Meditative Way, London, Darton, Longman & Todd, 1988; New York, Crossroad, 1988

The Inner Christ, London, Darton, Longman & Todd, 1987 (combines *Word into Silence*, *Moment of Christ* and *The Present Christ*)

Silence and Stillness in Every Season: Daily Readings with John Main, Paul Harris, Darton, Longman & Todd, 1997

The Present Christ: Further Steps in Meditation, London, Darton, Longman & Todd, 1985; New York, Crossroad, 1985

The Way of Unknowing: Expanding Spiritual Horizons through Meditation, London, Darton, Longman & Todd, 1989; New York, Crossroad, 1989

Word Made Flesh, ed. Laurence Freeman OSB, London, Darton, Longman & Todd, 1993; New York, Continuum, 1998

CDs/cassette tapes

The Life and Teachings of John Main, ed. Laurence Freeman OSB, Medio Media, 2002

Being on the Way, Medio Media, 1991

Christian Meditation: The Essential Teaching, Medio Media, 1991

Communitas, Volumes 1–5, Medio Media, 1991

Fully Alive, Medio Media, 1991

In the Beginning, Medio Media, 1991

The Christian Mysteries, Medio Media, 1979

The Door to Silence, Medio Media, 1985

The Last Conferences, Medio Media, 1991

Word Made Flesh, Medio Media, 1991

The World Community For Christian Meditation: Centres/Contacts Worldwide

For countries not listed contact International Centre.

International Centre
WCCM
St Mark's
Myddelton Square
London EC1R 1XX
UK
Tel: +44 20 7278 2070
Fax: +44 20 7713 6346
Email: mail@wccm.org
www.wccm.org

Australia
Australian Christian Meditation
    Community
PO Box 246
Uralla
New South Wales 2358
Australia
Tel: +61 2 9904 4638
Email: palmy@ozemail.com.au
www.christianmeditationaustralia.org

Belgium
Christelijk Meditatie Centrum
Beiaardlaan 1
B-1850 Grimbergen
Belgium
Tel/Fax: +32 2 305 7513
Email:ccm@pandora.be
www.christmed.be

Brazil
Comunidade de Meditacao
Crista
Caixa postal 62559
CEP 22252 Rio de Janeiro
Brasil
Tel: +55 21 2523 5125
Email: ana.fonseca@umusic.com
www.wccm.com.br

Canada
Christian Meditation
Community
Canadian National Resource
   Centre
P.O. Box 552, Station NDG
Montreal
Quebec H4A 3P9
Canada
Tel: +1 514 485 7928
Email:
ChristianMeditation@bellnet.ca
www.meditatio.ca

Méditation Chrétienne du
Québec
7400 boul. St Laurent, Suite 513
Montréal
Québec H2R 2Y1
Canada
Tel: +1 514 525 4649
Fax: +1 514 525 8110
Email: medchre@bellnet.ca
www.meditatio.ca

France
Communauté Mondiale de
   Méditants Chrétiens
126 rue Pelleport
75020 Paris
France
Tel: +33 1 40 31 89 73
Email: cmmc@wanadoo.fr
www.meditationchretienne.org

Germany
Zentrum für Christliche
   Meditation
Untere Leiten 12d
82065 Baierbrunn
Germany
Tel: +49 0 89680 20914
Email: Mariya@wccm.de
www.wccm.de

India
Christian Meditation Centre
Kripa Foundation
Mt Carmel Church
81/A Chapel Road
Bandra (W)
Mumbai 400050
India
Tel: +91 22 640 5411
Fax: + 91 22 643 9296
Email: frjoe@bom5.vsnl.net.in

Ireland
Christian Meditation Centre
4 Eblana Avenue
Dun Laoghaire
Co. Dublin
Ireland
Tel: +353 1 280 1505
Fax: +353 1 280 8720
Email: mclougf@hotmail.com
www.wccmireland.org

Italy
Comunità Mondiale per la
  Meditazione Cristiana
Via Marche, 2/a
25125 Brescia
Italy
Tel: +39 030 224549
Email: wccmitalia@virgilio.it
www.meditazionecristiana.org

Mexico
La Communidad Mundial de
  Meditacion Cristiana
Paseo de Golondrinas Closter
  11-401
C.P. 40880
Ixtapa, Guerrero
Mexico
Ubifone: 800-1320 1320
Tel: +52 755 55 3 01 20
Email: lucia_gayon@yahoo.com
www.meditacioncristiana.com

New Zealand
Christian Meditation
Community
PO Box 15-402
Tauranga
New Zealand
Tel: +64 7 544 7955
Email: stanman@xtra.co.nz

Singapore
Christian Meditation Centre
Church of the Holy Family
6 Chapel Road
Singapore 429509
Tel: +65 67376279
Email: daulet@pacific.net.sg
Tel: +65 64458062
Email: rebeccalim@pacific.net.sg
www.wccm.org/singapor.html

United Kingdom
London Christian Meditation
  Centre
St Mark's
Myddelton Square
London EC1R 1XX
UK
Tel: +44 20 7833 9615
Fax: +44 20 7713 6346
Email: uk@wccm.org
www.christian-meditation.org.
uk

USA
WCCM-US National
Information
  Center
627 N 6th Avenue
Tucson
Arizona 85705-8330
USA

Tel: +1 800 324 8305 / +1 520
882 0290
Fax: +1 520 882 0311
E-mail: meditate@mediomedia.
com
www.wccm-usa.org

About the World Community for Christian Meditation

The World Community for Christian Meditation took form in 1991. It continues John Main's legacy in teaching Christian meditation and his work of restoring the contemplation dimension of Christian faith in the life of the church.

The Community is now directed by Laurence Freeman OSB, a student of John Main and a Benedictine monk of the Olivetan Congregation. The World Community has its International Centre and a retreat centre in London. There are a number of centres in other parts of the world. The Community is thus a 'monastery without walls', a family of national communities and emerging communities in over a hundred countries. The foundation of this Community is the local meditation group, which meets weekly in homes, parishes, offices, hospitals, prisons and colleges. The World Community works closely with many Christian churches.

Annually it runs the John Main Seminar and The Way of Peace. It also sponsors retreats, schools for the training of teachers of meditation seminars, lectures and other programmes. It contributes to interfaith dialogues, and in recent years particularly with Buddhists and Muslims. A quarterly spiritual letter with news of the community is mailed and also available online. Weekly readings can be sent direct by email. Information on current programmes, connections to national co-ordinators and the location of meditation groups can be found on the Community website www.wccm.org, which also offers a range of online audio talks. This site is the hub of a growing internet family: the websites of national communities and special interests such as the teaching of meditation to children and the contemporary spirituality of priests.

Medio Media is the communication and publishing arm of The World Community and offers a wide range of books, audio material and videos to support the practice of meditation. The online bookstore is at www.mediomedia.org.